CALEB ROSS

Object-oriented Programming For game development

First edition

Contents

Introduction

Why Object-Oriented Programming in Game Development?

Object-Oriented Programming (OOP) is at the heart of modern software development, including game development. When we talk about OOP, we're not just focusing on programming techniques but on how these techniques facilitate creativity, efficiency, and scalability in game design. In an industry where complexity is continually increasing, with games needing to be more immersive, interactive, and feature-rich, having a solid programming paradigm is crucial.

OOP is designed to make complex software projects more manageable and intuitive, which is why it's highly applicable to game development. When building a game, you are working with various elements, like characters, objects, environments, physics, and AI systems. OOP allows you to treat these as *objects* with properties (attributes) and functionalities (methods). This mirroring of real-world entities and behaviors translates naturally into game development. It enables programmers to:

1. **Model Game Entities Effectively**: Characters, enemies, items, and other game elements can be modeled efficiently using classes, encapsulating their data and behaviors.
2. **Reusability**: Core classes like 'Player', 'NPC', or 'Weapon' can be reused

or inherited to create new variations without rewriting the entire code. This encourages modularity.

3. **Maintenance and Scalability**: Large games have thousands of moving parts. With OOP, each object functions semi-independently, making debugging, testing, and future expansions easier.

Additionally, OOP principles align closely with game engines and frameworks like Unity (which uses C#) and Unreal Engine (which uses C++). Understanding these principles equips you to utilize these powerful tools effectively, so you aren't just learning theoretical programming but gaining the ability to apply it practically in a professional development environment.

Overview of the Book

This book aims to take you from a foundational understanding of OOP to advanced techniques, specifically in the context of game development. Each chapter is structured to build on the knowledge gained from previous sections, ensuring a seamless progression from basic to complex game projects. You'll find real-world examples, case studies, and practical tutorials in each chapter to solidify your understanding.

Book Structure

Here's a brief outline of what you'll explore in this book:

- **Basics of OOP**: We'll start with understanding OOP concepts like classes, objects, inheritance, encapsulation, and polymorphism. You'll learn how these principles apply in creating characters, designing levels, and developing game mechanics.
- **Practical Projects**: Throughout the book, you'll build multiple game projects that increase in complexity, starting from basic mechanics to full-fledged 2D and 3D games. Each project is designed to demonstrate a unique application of OOP concepts.
- **Advanced OOP Techniques and Patterns**: You'll dive into more sophisticated techniques like design patterns and component-based

architecture. These techniques help organize code more efficiently, reduce errors, and enhance flexibility.

- **Cross-Platform Development**: As you gain confidence, you'll explore strategies for building games that can run on various platforms, focusing on maintaining code consistency and quality.
- **Optimizing and Debugging**: We'll discuss best practices for game performance optimization and debugging strategies to troubleshoot issues.

Each chapter comes with hands-on examples, and at the end of the book, you'll have completed several game projects, each emphasizing specific OOP concepts and patterns.

What You'll Learn and Build

The primary goal of this book is to teach you to harness the power of OOP to create games. However, we aim to go beyond mere syntax and code by providing you with insights into game development strategies, techniques, and principles. Here's a snapshot of what you'll learn:

1. **Foundational Knowledge of OOP Principles**: You'll start with understanding the basic principles of OOP—what they are, why they matter, and how they translate to game development. Concepts like classes, objects, inheritance, polymorphism, and encapsulation will be covered in-depth, with practical game-related examples.
2. **Applying OOP Concepts to Game Development**: You'll learn how to create classes for game characters, enemies, and game elements. For instance, you'll implement polymorphism to create variations of enemies with shared behaviors or inheritance to expand on base classes.
3. **Building Core Game Mechanics**: You'll create game projects that implement essential mechanics like player movement, enemy AI, power-ups, and interactive elements. Each project reinforces a different OOP principle.

4. **Advanced OOP Design Patterns**: Understanding and applying design patterns is crucial for efficient coding. We'll explore patterns like Singleton for managing game states, Factory for creating objects dynamically, Observer for handling events, and more. You'll learn how to incorporate these patterns into your game projects.

5. **Handling User Interfaces**: Designing user interfaces like HUDs, menus, and pop-ups using OOP principles ensures that your UI elements are modular, manageable, and scalable. You'll implement interactive menus, health bars, and inventory screens.

6. **Cross-Platform Development Techniques**: Writing maintainable code that runs on multiple platforms (like Windows, iOS, and Android) requires foresight and strategic class design. We'll cover techniques to make your code platform-agnostic.

7. **Optimizing and Debugging OOP Code**: Writing efficient OOP code is just one part of game development. You'll also learn how to identify and fix common performance bottlenecks, memory leaks, and logical errors.

8. **Advanced Topics and Future Trends**: We'll explore cutting-edge topics like component-based design, AI programming with OOP, and trends in modern game development using machine learning and procedural generation.

By the end of this book, you'll not only be able to write clean, efficient, and scalable OOP-based code but also be equipped with the mindset and practical experience to tackle new and more complex projects.

Who This Book is For

Before diving into the chapters, it's essential to understand who will benefit the most from this book. Here's a breakdown of the target audience:

- **Aspiring Game Developers**: If you're interested in making games and want to build a solid programming foundation, this book is for you. You don't need prior game development experience, but basic programming knowledge would be helpful.

- **Junior and Intermediate Programmers**: For those who have a basic understanding of programming and are looking to specialize in game development, this book provides a clear path to mastering OOP in a game development context.
- **Indie Game Developers**: If you're an indie developer looking to refine your coding techniques and structure your projects more efficiently, this book offers advanced OOP concepts and best practices tailored to game development.
- **Students and Educators**: Computer science students or educators will find this book an excellent resource for learning or teaching the application of OOP principles in a real-world, practical way through game development.

Prerequisites and Tools

To fully benefit from this book, there are some fundamental skills and tools you'll need:

Prerequisites

- **Basic Programming Knowledge**: You should have a basic understanding of programming concepts like variables, loops, and functions. If you have experience with languages like C#, C++, or Python, you'll find it easier to follow along.
- **Familiarity with a Game Engine**: Although not mandatory, familiarity with game engines like Unity, Unreal Engine, or Godot would be beneficial. This book will offer an introduction to these engines, but prior experience will help you grasp the topics faster.

Tools

Throughout this book, we'll be using specific tools and software to write and test our game code. Here's a list of essential tools:

1. **Integrated Development Environment (IDE)**: You'll need an IDE to write and run your code. For example, if you're using C# with Unity, Visual Studio or Visual Studio Code would be the ideal choice. For Unreal Engine with C++, Visual Studio is also highly recommended.
2. **Game Engines**: We'll focus primarily on Unity and Unreal Engine due to their widespread use and robust support for OOP principles. You can download these engines for free:

- **Unity**: A powerful and versatile engine that's beginner-friendly and excellent for learning OOP through C#.
- **Unreal Engine**: Known for its advanced graphics capabilities and C++ programming, Unreal is a great choice for those looking to delve deeper into the mechanics of game development.

1. **Version Control**: Using version control like Git is recommended, especially when working on game projects. It helps in tracking changes and managing projects collaboratively if needed. GitHub or GitLab are popular choices.
2. **Asset Creation Tools**: Although this book focuses on programming, having basic knowledge of creating or sourcing game assets like sprites, 3D models, and audio files will enhance your game projects. Tools like Blender, GIMP, or Photoshop for visuals and Audacity for audio are great options.
3. **Other Utilities**: Depending on your chosen engine and project complexity, other tools like physics simulation libraries or input management plugins might be useful.

Chapter 1: Understanding Object-Oriented Programming Basics

The Core Principles: Classes, Objects, Inheritance, Polymorphism, Encapsulation

O bject-Oriented Programming (OOP) is one of the most widely used programming paradigms in the world of software development. It mirrors the way we perceive the world by breaking down complex entities into smaller, manageable parts—objects. In game development, the principles of OOP help developers create a framework that's not only easy to build and maintain but also more intuitive for visualizing game elements.

In this section, we'll explore the core principles of OOP and how they provide a foundation for understanding more advanced topics later in the book.

1. Classes and Objects

In Object-Oriented Programming, the fundamental building blocks are classes and objects. These concepts form the backbone of how you think about structuring your code.

1.1. Classes: The Blueprint of Objects

A class is essentially a blueprint or a template that defines the structure and behavior of an object. Think of a class as a mold used to create multiple objects of the same kind. It encapsulates the attributes (properties) and methods (functions) of the entity it represents. Let's consider an example from game development:

Imagine you're building a game with multiple types of characters, such as knights, wizards, and archers. You can create a class called Character that serves as a blueprint for all the characters in your game.

```csharp
Copy code
class Character
{
    public string Name;
    public int Health;
    public int Stamina;

    public void Attack()
    {
        Console.WriteLine($"{Name} attacks the enemy!");
    }

    public void Defend()
    {
        Console.WriteLine($"{Name} defends against the attack!");
    }
}
```

This Character class defines attributes like Name, Health, and Stamina, and behaviors like Attack() and Defend(). The class doesn't yet represent a specific character in the game—it's just a template.

1.2. Objects: Instances of Classes

An object is an instance of a class. It represents a specific entity that's created based on the class blueprint. Continuing our example, you can create multiple characters (objects) from the Character class.

```csharp
Copy code
Character knight = new Character();
knight.Name = "Arthur";
knight.Health = 100;
knight.Stamina = 50;

Character wizard = new Character();
wizard.Name = "Merlin";
wizard.Health = 80;
wizard.Stamina = 70;
```

Here, knight and wizard are objects, each with their own specific values for the Name, Health, and Stamina attributes. Although they share the same class, their properties can vary, allowing you to create diverse characters in your game.

2. Inheritance

Inheritance is a powerful OOP principle that allows one class to inherit the attributes and behaviors of another class. It promotes code reuse and helps in creating a hierarchy of classes, which is particularly useful in game development.

2.1. Understanding Inheritance

In inheritance, you define a base class that contains common attributes and methods. Other classes, known as derived or child classes, can inherit these properties and extend them to add new attributes or modify existing ones. Let's expand on our previous example by creating specific classes for different types of characters:

```csharp
Copy code
class Knight : Character
{
    public int Armor;
```

```
    public void ShieldBlock()
    {
        Console.WriteLine($"{Name} blocks the attack with a
        shield!");
    }
}

class Wizard : Character
{
    public int Mana;

    public void CastSpell()
    {
        Console.WriteLine($"{Name} casts a powerful spell!");
    }
}
```

In this example, the Knight and Wizard classes inherit from the base Character class. They share the attributes and methods of the base class (Name, Health, Attack(), and Defend()), but they also introduce new attributes (Armor and Mana) and behaviors (ShieldBlock() and CastSpell()).

This is a practical way to represent different characters in a game without duplicating code. By creating a hierarchy of classes, you can easily add new types of characters without rewriting existing logic.

2.2. How Inheritance Promotes Flexibility

The inheritance model offers several advantages in game development:

- **Code Reusability**: You can define common attributes and methods in a base class and reuse them across multiple derived classes. This reduces redundancy and makes code easier to maintain.
- **Extensibility**: Inheritance allows you to extend or override the base class methods in derived classes, providing flexibility to modify or enhance character behavior.

3. Polymorphism

Polymorphism is an OOP principle that allows you to use a single interface or method in different ways. It enables objects to take on multiple forms, promoting flexibility and scalability in your code.

3.1. Method Overloading and Overriding

There are two main types of polymorphism: method overloading and method overriding.

- **Method Overloading**: This involves creating multiple methods with the same name but different parameters. For example, you might have a CastSpell() method that accepts different types of spells:

```csharp
Copy code
class Wizard : Character
{
    public int Mana;

    public void CastSpell(string spellName)
    {
        Console.WriteLine($"{Name} casts {spellName}!");
    }

    public void CastSpell(string spellName, int spellPower)
    {
        Console.WriteLine($"{Name} casts {spellName} with power
        {spellPower}!");
    }
}
```

- **Method Overriding**: This involves overriding a base class method in a derived class to provide a different implementation. For example, the Attack() method in the Knight class might involve swinging a sword, while the Attack() method in the Wizard class involves casting a spell.

```csharp
Copy code
class Knight : Character
{
    public override void Attack()
    {
        Console.WriteLine($"{Name} swings a sword at the enemy!");
    }
}

class Wizard : Character
{
    public override void Attack()
    {
        Console.WriteLine($"{Name} casts a fireball at the
        enemy!");
    }
}
```

Here, both the Knight and Wizard classes override the base class Attack() method to provide different behaviors. This is a simple example of polymorphism in action.

3.2. How Polymorphism Improves Code Organization

Polymorphism allows you to write flexible and scalable code in game development. It promotes consistency in method names while allowing different behaviors based on the object's type. This is particularly useful when you're dealing with various characters or items in a game that share common methods but exhibit different behaviors.

4. Encapsulation

Encapsulation is the principle of hiding the internal details of an object and providing controlled access to its attributes and methods. This is achieved using access modifiers like private, protected, and public.

4.1. Protecting Object Data

In game development, encapsulation helps protect an object's data from being directly modified by external code. Instead, you provide public methods to get or set values while keeping the actual data hidden. This ensures that the object's state remains consistent and reduces the risk of accidental errors.

```csharp
Copy code
class Character
{
    private int health;

    public int Health
    {
        get { return health; }
        set
        {
            if (value > 0)
            {
                health = value;
            }
        }
    }

    public void TakeDamage(int damage)
    {
        health -= damage;
        Console.WriteLine($"{Name} takes {damage} damage!
        Remaining health: {health}");
    }
}
```

In this example, the health attribute is private, meaning it can only be accessed or modified through the public Health property or methods like TakeDamage(). This approach prevents external code from setting the health value to an invalid number, ensuring that your game logic remains stable.

4.2. Benefits of Encapsulation in Game Development

Encapsulation offers several key benefits for game developers:

- **Data Protection**: It safeguards the internal state of an object, reducing the risk of accidental modifications.
- **Code Maintenance**: Encapsulation makes it easier to change the internal implementation of a class without affecting other parts of the code. This promotes modularity and scalability.

How OOP Applies to Game Development

In game development, OOP principles are not just theoretical—they provide a practical way to model and manage complex systems within a game. Let's explore how OOP applies specifically to game development:

1. Modeling Game Entities

Games are built around a variety of entities, such as characters, items, environments, and interactive objects. OOP allows you to model these entities as classes, with each class representing a specific type of game entity.

For example, in a role-playing game (RPG), you might have classes like Player, Enemy, Item, and Weapon. Each of these classes can have its own attributes and behaviors, encapsulated within the class. This mirrors the real-world concept of objects, making it easier to understand and organize game code.

2. Managing Complexity with Inheritance

In large games, you often have multiple variations of a common entity. Inheritance allows you to create a hierarchy of classes that share common attributes and behaviors while adding new features in derived classes.

For instance, in a game with different types of enemies, you can define a base class called Enemy and create derived classes like Goblin, Orc, and Dragon. This way, you can avoid duplicating code while maintaining the unique characteristics of each enemy type.

3. Flexibility with Polymorphism

Polymorphism allows you to design flexible code that can work with different types of objects in a consistent way. In a game, this might involve creating a method called Interact() that applies to all game objects, such as characters, items, and NPCs. Each object can have its own implementation of the Interact() method, enabling unique interactions for each type of object.

4. Encapsulation for Robustness and Security

Encapsulation plays a crucial role in protecting the internal state of game objects. In a game, objects like characters or items have various properties that need to be safeguarded to prevent unintended modifications. Encapsulation ensures that these properties are only accessible or modifiable through controlled methods.

The Importance of OOP in Game Architecture

Game architecture refers to the overall structure and organization of your game's code. A well-architected game is easier to develop, debug, maintain, and expand. OOP provides a solid framework for creating organized, modular, and maintainable game architectures. Let's explore why OOP is crucial for game architecture:

1. Modular Design and Code Reusability

OOP promotes a modular design approach, where each class or object represents a specific part of the game. This modularity enables code reuse, as you can create reusable components that can be easily integrated into new projects. For example, if you develop a robust Inventory class for one game, you can reuse it in future games with minimal modifications.

2. Scalability for Large Games

As games grow in size and complexity, managing the codebase becomes increasingly challenging. OOP helps you scale your code by breaking it down into smaller, self-contained objects. This reduces interdependencies between different parts of the code, making it easier to add new features or modify existing ones.

3. Enhanced Debugging and Testing

OOP improves the debugging and testing process by allowing you to isolate and test individual classes or objects. This isolation makes it easier to identify and fix bugs, as well as perform unit tests on specific components of the game. Additionally, encapsulation helps ensure that changes to one part of the code don't inadvertently affect other parts.

4. Improved Collaboration in Game Development

In game development teams, multiple developers often work on different aspects of the game simultaneously. OOP facilitates collaboration by providing a clear structure and defined interfaces for different parts of the game. Each developer can work on specific classes or objects without worrying about conflicts or dependencies.

This chapter covers the core principles of OOP and their application in game development. It introduces readers to classes, objects, inheritance, polymorphism, and encapsulation, laying the foundation for the rest of the book. By understanding these principles, readers will be better equipped to design and build their own game projects using OOP techniques.

Chapter 2: Getting Started with Game Development Frameworks

As you embark on your journey into game development, choosing the right development framework is essential. Game frameworks, particularly game engines, provide all the tools you need to design, create, and deploy your games. In this chapter, we will explore the basics of setting up a development environment, the most popular game engines available, choosing the right programming language for your project, and finally, creating a simple "Hello World" project in each of the chosen engines.

By the end of this chapter, you will have a foundational understanding of how to set up and begin working with game development frameworks.

Section 1: Setting Up Your Development Environment

Before you start building games, it's crucial to have the correct development environment set up. A well-configured environment ensures that you have all the necessary tools, libraries, and settings to code efficiently without technical interruptions.

1.1 Choosing Your Platform and Software

Operating Systems

Most game development frameworks are compatible with Windows, macOS, and Linux. The choice of operating system will depend largely on the game engine you choose. For example:

- **Unity and Unreal Engine** both support Windows and macOS fully. Unity has good support for Linux as well.
- **Godot Engine** supports Windows, macOS, and Linux natively, making it an excellent choice for those who prefer open-source software.

Development Environment Software

- **Code Editors**: You'll need an Integrated Development Environment (IDE) or a code editor to write and manage your game's code. Popular options include:
- **Visual Studio** (best for C# development in Unity or C++ in Unreal Engine).
- **Visual Studio Code** (lightweight and versatile for various programming languages).
- **Rider** by JetBrains (especially recommended for Unity development).
- **IntelliJ IDEA** for those who prefer a broader development toolkit.
- **Version Control**: It's a good practice to use a version control system like **Git**. Version control helps you manage your project's changes, collaborate with team members, and avoid losing work.

1.2 Installing Essential Tools

1. **Download and Install Git**
2. If you're not familiar with version control, Git is a great starting point. You can use GitHub, GitLab, or Bitbucket as hosting platforms. Install Git from the official site (git-scm.com) and set up a GitHub account if you don't have one.

3. **Installing a Code Editor**
4. Choose a code editor that aligns with your engine and language choice. For example, if you're working with Unity, Visual Studio or Rider might be the best fit.
5. **Configuring a Game Engine**
6. Depending on the engine you choose (Unity, Unreal, or Godot), install the necessary software and follow the installation instructions. For example:

- For Unity, you'll need **Unity Hub** to manage your Unity installations, projects, and licenses.
- For Unreal Engine, download the **Epic Games Launcher** and install Unreal Engine from there.
- For Godot, download the latest version directly from the Godot website, as it's a single executable file without any installation hassle.

Section 2: Overview of Game Engines (Unity, Unreal, Godot)

Choosing the right game engine is vital to your success in game development. Each engine has its own strengths, weaknesses, and unique features. Let's dive into the three most popular engines and understand what makes them the top choices for developers worldwide.

2.1 Unity Engine

2.1.1 What is Unity?

Unity is a highly popular and versatile game engine known for its user-friendly interface and extensive cross-platform capabilities. It supports a wide range of platforms, including PC, consoles, mobile, VR, and even AR devices. Unity's programming language is **C#**, which is easy to learn and powerful enough to develop complex game mechanics.

2.1.2 Key Features of Unity

- **Cross-Platform Development**: Build games for over 25 platforms, including Windows, macOS, Android, iOS, PlayStation, Xbox, and more.
- **Asset Store**: Unity's Asset Store is a marketplace for purchasing or downloading free 3D models, textures, audio files, scripts, and more.
- **Visual Scripting**: Unity provides a visual scripting tool called **Bolt**, which allows you to create complex behaviors without writing a single line of code.
- **Ease of Use**: Unity's editor is user-friendly, making it a preferred choice for beginners and experienced developers alike.

2.1.3 What Type of Games Can You Create?

With Unity, you can create 2D and 3D games, as well as AR/VR applications. The engine is versatile enough to handle simple mobile games, complex multiplayer games, and stunning VR experiences.

2.2 Unreal Engine

2.2.1 What is Unreal Engine?

Developed by Epic Games, Unreal Engine is a powerful game development framework known for its exceptional graphical capabilities. It's widely used in AAA game development and offers advanced features for building realistic 3D games. Unreal Engine uses **C++** as its primary programming language but also offers **Blueprints**, a visual scripting system that makes it accessible for non-programmers.

2.2.2 Key Features of Unreal Engine

- **Advanced Graphics and Visuals**: Unreal Engine is known for its top-tier graphical capabilities, including real-time ray tracing and physically-based rendering.
- **Blueprint Visual Scripting**: Unreal's visual scripting system allows you to create game logic without writing code, making it easier for artists and designers to contribute to the development process.
- **Extensive Asset Library**: Epic's Marketplace offers a wealth of assets,

plugins, and tools to accelerate game development.
- **Full Source Code Access**: With Unreal, you have full access to the engine's source code, enabling deep customization and optimization.

2.2.3 What Type of Games Can You Create?

Unreal Engine is ideal for creating high-quality 3D games, including AAA titles, realistic simulations, and VR/AR experiences. It's widely used in the industry for first-person shooters, RPGs, and open-world games.

2.3 Godot Engine

2.3.1 What is Godot?

Godot is a free and open-source game engine that is gaining popularity due to its lightweight design and simplicity. It supports both 2D and 3D game development and uses its own scripting language called **GDScript**, which is similar to Python. Godot is highly customizable and community-driven.

2.3.2 Key Features of Godot

- **2D and 3D Capabilities**: Godot offers dedicated 2D and 3D engines, making it suitable for a wide range of game genres.
- **Open-Source and Lightweight**: Godot is entirely open-source, allowing developers to customize the engine to fit their needs.
- **Simple Scripting with GDScript**: GDScript is a lightweight scripting language similar to Python, making it easy to learn and use.
- **Node-Based Architecture**: Godot uses a node-based scene system that promotes modularity and reuse.

2.3.3 What Type of Games Can You Create?

Godot is well-suited for 2D games, small to medium-sized 3D games, and experimental projects. It's an excellent choice for developers looking to get started with game development without the overhead of heavy engine requirements.

Section 3: Choosing the Right Language for Your Project

3.1 Factors to Consider When Choosing a Language

When selecting a programming language for your game development project, consider the following factors:

1. **Game Engine Compatibility**: The language must be compatible with your chosen game engine. For example:

- Unity uses **C#**.
- Unreal Engine uses **C++** and **Blueprints**.
- Godot primarily uses **GDScript**, but it also supports **C#**, **VisualScript**, and **C++**.

1. **Project Requirements**: If you're building a complex game with heavy calculations or advanced graphics, you might prefer a language with better performance and control, such as **C++** in Unreal Engine. If you're building a simple mobile game, **C#** in Unity or **GDScript** in Godot could be the better choice.
2. **Ease of Learning**: Choose a language that matches your skill level. **C#** and **GDScript** are beginner-friendly, while **C++** is more challenging but offers greater control.

3.2 Overview of Common Game Development Languages

C#

C# is the primary language used in Unity. It's known for its simplicity and strong community support. C# is object-oriented, making it a great choice for developers who are new to game development. It offers a rich set of features that make managing game objects, behaviors, and systems more efficient.

C++

C++ is the go-to language for Unreal Engine developers. It's a powerful language that provides low-level control over memory and performance. While C++ is more challenging to learn, it's an excellent choice for developers who want to optimize their game's performance and work on AAA-level games.

GDScript

GDScript is a high-level scripting language used in Godot Engine. It's designed to be simple, easy to read, and similar to Python. GDScript allows you to create and manage game objects without diving into complex syntax, making it an ideal choice for beginners.

Section 4: Hello World in Your Chosen Game Engine

The "Hello World" program is often the first step in learning a new programming language or framework. In game development, creating a simple "Hello World" project in your chosen game engine helps you get comfortable with the engine's interface and scripting.

4.1 Hello World in Unity (Using C#)

1. **Create a New Unity Project**

- Open Unity Hub and create a new project. Select the **3D** or **2D** template based on your preference.
- Name your project (e.g., "HelloWorldUnity") and choose a location to save it.

1. **Add a 3D Object to the Scene**

- In the Unity Editor, go to the **Hierarchy** window and right-click. Choose **3D Object > Cube** to add a cube to the scene.

1. **Create a C# Script**

- In the **Assets** folder, right-click and choose **Create > C# Script**. Name the script "HelloWorldScript".
- Double-click the script to open it in Visual Studio or your preferred code editor. Edit the script as follows:

```csharp
Copy code
using UnityEngine;

public class HelloWorldScript : MonoBehaviour
{
    void Start()
    {
        Debug.Log("Hello, World!");
    }
}
```

1. **Attach the Script to the Cube**

- In the Unity Editor, select the **Cube** object in the **Hierarchy** window.
- Drag the **HelloWorldScript** from the **Assets** folder to the **Inspector** window to attach it to the cube.

1. **Run the Game**

- Click the **Play** button at the top of the Unity Editor. You should see "Hello, World!" printed in the **Console** window.

4.2 Hello World in Unreal Engine (Using C++)

1. **Create a New Unreal Project**

- Open the **Epic Games Launcher** and launch **Unreal Engine**. Create a

new project using the **Blank** template and select **Blueprint/C++** based on your preference.
- Name your project (e.g., "HelloWorldUnreal") and choose a location to save it.

1. **Create a C++ Class**

- In the **Content Browser**, right-click and choose **New C++ Class**. Select **Actor** as the base class and name it "HelloWorldActor".

1. **Edit the C++ Class**

- Open the **HelloWorldActor.cpp** file in Visual Studio. Add the following code to the BeginPlay method:

```cpp
Copy code
void AHelloWorldActor::BeginPlay()
{
    Super::BeginPlay();
    UE_LOG(LogTemp, Warning, TEXT("Hello, World!"));
}
```

1. **Compile and Add the Actor to the Scene**

- Compile the code and return to the Unreal Editor. Drag the **HelloWorl-dActor** into the scene.
- Click the **Play** button to run the project. You should see "Hello, World!" printed in the **Output Log**.

4.3 Hello World in Godot (Using GDScript)

1. **Create a New Godot Project**

- Open **Godot Engine** and create a new project. Choose a location and name the project (e.g., "HelloWorldGodot").

1. **Add a Node to the Scene**

- In the **Scene** tab, click + to add a new node. Choose **2D Scene** as the root node.

1. **Create a GDScript**

- Right-click the **2D Scene** node and choose **Attach Script**. Name the script "HelloWorldScript".
- Edit the script as follows:

```gdscript
Copy code
extends Node2D

func _ready():
    print("Hello, World!")
```

1. **Run the Scene**

- Save the scene and click the **Play** button. You should see "Hello, World!" printed in the **Output** window.

In this chapter, we've covered the essential aspects of setting up your development environment, choosing a game engine, selecting a programming language, and creating your first simple project. With a solid foundation in place, you're now ready to dive deeper into the world of game development. From here, you can start exploring more advanced concepts, building more complex projects, and refining your skills.

Chapter 3: Building Your First Game: Applying OOP Concepts

Building a game requires more than just coding. It involves designing systems, understanding relationships between game objects, and translating real-world logic into code. In this chapter, we will create a simple game using Object-Oriented Programming (OOP) principles. We'll focus on establishing basic game mechanics and building solid foundations with reusable and maintainable code.

Section 1: Creating a Simple Game: Building Blocks with OOP

The objective of this section is to understand how to conceptualize and develop a simple game using the fundamentals of OOP. For our project, let's create a straightforward 2D game: *"Space Defender"*. The player controls a spaceship, and the objective is to eliminate incoming enemy ships.

1.1 Game Overview

In *Space Defender*, you have:

- A **player-controlled spaceship** that can move and shoot.
- **Enemy ships** that spawn at random intervals and move toward the

player.
- **Projectiles** fired by the player to destroy the enemies.
- A **simple score system** to track the player's success.

We will break down these elements using OOP principles by defining appropriate classes and methods.

1.2 Establishing Core Classes

1.2.1 Why Classes Matter

Classes represent the blueprint for game objects. Each core element in the game—such as the player, enemies, projectiles, and environment—can be encapsulated within a class. This modularity helps organize and manage complex systems more effectively.

1.2.2 Core Classes in Space Defender

For *Space Defender*, the key classes we'll create are:

- **Player**: Represents the player-controlled spaceship.
- **Enemy**: Represents enemy ships that try to attack the player.
- **Projectile**: Represents the bullets or lasers fired by the player.
- **GameManager**: Manages the overall game state, score, and level progression.

We'll define these classes and outline their attributes and behaviors in the following sections.

Section 2: Defining Game Classes: Player, Enemy, Environment

2.1 Designing the Player Class

The player class represents the spaceship controlled by the player. Let's define its basic structure and responsibilities.

2.1.1 Attributes of the Player Class

- **Position**: The X and Y coordinates of the player's spaceship.
- **Speed**: The movement speed of the spaceship.
- **Health**: The amount of damage the spaceship can take before being destroyed.
- **ProjectileType**: The type of projectile the player can shoot.

2.1.2 Methods of the Player Class

- **Move()**: Allows the player to move the spaceship left, right, up, or down.
- **Shoot()**: Creates and fires a projectile.
- **TakeDamage()**: Reduces the player's health when hit by an enemy projectile.

Here's a basic implementation of the Player class in C# (for Unity):

```csharp
Copy code
public class Player : MonoBehaviour
{
    public float speed = 5f;
    public int health = 100;
    public GameObject projectilePrefab;

    void Update()
    {
```

```
        Move();
        if (Input.GetKeyDown(KeyCode.Space))
        {
            Shoot();
        }
    }

    void Move()
    {
        float horizontal = Input.GetAxis("Horizontal") * speed *
        Time.deltaTime;
        float vertical = Input.
GetAxis("Vertical") * speed * Time.deltaTime;
        transform.Translate(new
  Vector3(horizontal, vertical, 0));
    }

    void Shoot()
    {
        Instantiate(projectilePrefab, transform.position,
        Quaternion.identity);
    }

    public void TakeDamage(int damage)
    {
        health -= damage;
        if (health <= 0)
        {
            Destroy(gameObject); // Destroys the player object
        }
    }
}
```

This script demonstrates the basic movement and shooting mechanics of the player.

2.2 Designing the Enemy Class

The enemy class represents the hostile ships that the player needs to destroy.

2.2.1 Attributes of the Enemy Class

- **Position**: The X and Y coordinates of the enemy ship.
- **Speed**: The movement speed of the enemy ship.
- **Health**: The amount of damage the enemy can take before being destroyed.
- **Damage**: The amount of damage the enemy deals to the player.

2.2.2 Methods of the Enemy Class

- **Move()**: Moves the enemy toward the player.
- **TakeDamage()**: Reduces the enemy's health when hit by a projectile.
- **AttackPlayer()**: Decreases the player's health on collision.

Here's a basic implementation of the Enemy class in C#:

```csharp
Copy code
public class Enemy : MonoBehaviour
{
    public float speed = 2f;
    public int health = 50;
    public int damage = 20;

    void Update()
    {
        Move();
    }

    void Move()
    {
        transform.Translate(Vector3.down *
```

```
speed * Time.deltaTime);
    }

    public void TakeDamage(int damageAmount)
    {
        health -= damageAmount;
        if (health <= 0)
        {
            Destroy(gameObject);
        }
    }

    private void OnCollisionEnter2D
(Collision2D collision)
    {
        if (collision.gameObject.tag == "Player")
        {
            collision.gameObject.
GetComponent<Player>().TakeDamage(damage);
            Destroy(gameObject);
        }
    }
}
```

This script makes the enemy move toward the bottom of the screen and damages the player on collision.

2.3 Designing the Projectile Class

The projectile class represents the bullets or lasers fired by the player.

2.3.1 Attributes of the Projectile Class

- **Position**: The starting position of the projectile.
- **Speed**: The speed of the projectile.
- **Damage**: The amount of damage the projectile deals to enemies.

2.3.2 Methods of the Projectile Class

- **Move()**: Moves the projectile forward.
- **OnCollision()**: Handles collisions with enemies.

Here's a basic implementation of the Projectile class in C#:

```csharp
Copy code
public class Projectile : MonoBehaviour
{
    public float speed = 10f;
    public int damage = 10;

    void Update()
    {
        Move();
    }

    void Move()
    {
        transform.Translate(Vector3.up *
speed * Time.deltaTime);
    }

    private void OnTriggerEnter2D
(Collider2D collision)
    {
if (collision.gameObject.tag == "Enemy")
        {
            collision.gameObject.
GetComponent<Enemy>().
TakeDamage(damage);
            Destroy(gameObject);
// Destroy the projectile after hitting the enemy
        }
    }
}
```

This script moves the projectile upwards and damages enemies on collision.

2.4 Designing the GameManager Class

The GameManager class manages the overall game state, score, and game flow.

2.4.1 Responsibilities of the GameManager Class

- **Managing the Score**: Keeping track of the player's score.
- **Spawning Enemies**: Spawning enemies at random intervals.
- **Handling Game Over**: Ending the game when the player's health reaches zero.

Here's a basic implementation of the GameManager class in C#:

```csharp
Copy code
public class GameManager : MonoBehaviour
{
    public int score = 0;
    public GameObject enemyPrefab;
    public Transform[] spawnPoints;
    public float spawnInterval = 3f;

    void Start()
    {
        InvokeRepeating("SpawnEnemy",
spawnInterval, spawnInterval);
    }

    void SpawnEnemy()
    {
        int spawnIndex = Random.Range
(0, spawnPoints.Length);
        Instantiate(enemyPrefab,
spawnPoints[spawnIndex].position,
Quaternion.identity);
    }
```

```
public void AddScore(int points)
{
    score += points;
}
}
```

This script spawns enemies at random intervals and keeps track of the player's score.

Section 3: Object Relationships and Communication

3.1 Establishing Object Interactions

In game development, objects need to communicate and interact with each other to create meaningful gameplay. Object relationships involve establishing how different classes interact within the game.

3.2 Communication Between Objects

Communication between objects is crucial. For example:

- When a **projectile** hits an **enemy**, it needs to reduce the enemy's health and potentially destroy the enemy.
- When an **enemy** collides with the **player**, it should deal damage to the player and possibly destroy itself.

3.2.1 Messaging and Events

In OOP, objects communicate through messages (method calls) and events. For instance:

- A Projectile object might call the TakeDamage() method on an Enemy object.
- An Enemy might invoke an event on collision to notify the GameManager

about the player taking damage.

3.3 Implementing Object Relationships in Code

Here's an example of how communication works between the Projectile, Enemy, and Player classes in Unity:

```csharp
Copy code
// Inside Projectile.cs
private void OnTriggerEnter2D
(Collider2D collision)
{
    if (collision.gameObject.tag == "Enemy")
    {
        collision.gameObject.GetComponent<Enemy>().TakeDamage(damage);
        Destroy(gameObject);
    }
}
```

```csharp
Copy code
// Inside Enemy.cs
private void OnCollisionEnter2D
(Collision2D collision)
{
    if (collision.gameObject.tag == "Player")
    {
        collision.gameObject.GetComponent<Player>().TakeDamage(damage);
        Destroy(gameObject);
    }
}
```

By using tags, method calls, and component references, we establish clear communication between objects.

Section 4: Expanding on Simple Game Mechanics

4.1 Enhancing the Game with New Mechanics

Now that we have the basic game structure in place, let's expand on the mechanics to make the game more engaging. Here are a few ideas to add depth to our simple game:

- **Power-Ups**: Create power-ups that temporarily boost the player's health, speed, or firepower.
- **Advanced Enemy AI**: Implement more sophisticated enemy movement patterns or attacks.
- **Level Progression**: Design multiple levels with increasing difficulty.

4.2 Implementing Power-Ups

Let's define a PowerUp class that grants a temporary boost to the player:

```csharp
Copy code
public class PowerUp : MonoBehaviour
{
    public string powerUpType;
    public float duration = 5f;

    private void OnTriggerEnter2D(Collider2D collision)
    {
        if (collision.gameObject.tag == "Player")
        {
            if (powerUpType == "Health")
            {
                collision.gameObject.
GetComponent<Player>().health += 50;
            }
            else if (powerUpType == "Speed")
            {
                StartCoroutine(BoostSpeed
(collision.gameObject));
```

```
            }

            Destroy(gameObject);
// Destroy the power-up after being collected
        }
    }

    private IEnumerator BoostSpeed(GameObject player)
    {
        Player playerScript = player.
GetComponent<Player>();
        playerScript.speed *= 2;
        yield return new WaitForSeconds(duration);
        playerScript.speed /= 2;
    }
}
```

This script implements two types of power-ups: health boosts and speed boosts.

4.3 Implementing Level Progression

We can enhance the GameManager class to handle level progression based on the player's score:

```csharp
Copy code
public class GameManager : MonoBehaviour
{
    public int score = 0;
    public int currentLevel = 1;
    public int scoreToNextLevel = 100;

    void Update()
    {
        if (score >= scoreToNextLevel)
        {
            AdvanceToNextLevel();
```

```
        }
    }

    void AdvanceToNextLevel()
    {
        currentLevel++;
        scoreToNextLevel += 100;
        spawnInterval -= 0.5f;
    }
}
```

This script increases the difficulty of the game as the player advances to higher levels.

Conclusion

In this chapter, we built a simple game using Object-Oriented Programming principles. We started by defining core classes for key game objects, establishing their attributes and behaviors. We then focused on implementing object relationships and communication, allowing our game objects to interact meaningfully.

By understanding and applying OOP concepts, you can create more organized, modular, and scalable game projects. As you move forward, consider experimenting with new mechanics and refining the code to gain deeper insights into the power of OOP in game development.

Chapter 4: Advanced Class Design and Game Structure

As you advance in your game development journey, understanding how to design and structure your game code becomes increasingly important. Object-oriented programming (OOP) concepts like class hierarchies, inheritance, and composition play significant roles in helping you manage complexity, maintain scalability, and enhance the flexibility of your game's codebase.

This chapter will guide you through advanced techniques in class design and game structure, using practical examples and clear explanations.

Section 1: Class Hierarchies and Inheritance in Game Development

Class hierarchies and inheritance allow game developers to model complex relationships between different entities in a game. By designing a hierarchy, you can share common attributes and behaviors among related classes, making the code more organized and reducing redundancy.

1.1 Understanding Class Hierarchies

A class hierarchy is a system in which classes are organized in a parent-child (or base-derived) relationship. The base class defines common attributes and methods, while the derived classes extend or modify this behavior as needed.

1.1.1 Why Class Hierarchies Matter in Game Development

In game development, you'll often deal with various types of game entities that share similar behaviors. For instance, in an action-adventure game, you may have different kinds of NPCs (Non-Playable Characters) like merchants, enemies, and neutral characters. All these entities share common properties like position, health, and dialogue options but have specific behaviors unique to their type.

1.1.2 Building a Class Hierarchy

Let's consider a simple RPG-style game that involves a base class for NPCs and several derived classes:

- **Base Class**: NPC
- **Derived Classes**: Merchant, Enemy, Neutral

Here's an example using C#:

```csharp
Copy code
// Base Class: NPC
public class NPC
{
    public string Name;
    public int Health;
    public Vector2 Position;

    public virtual void Speak()
    {
        Debug.Log($"{Name} says: Hello, adventurer!");
    }
}
```

```
// Derived Class: Merchant
public class Merchant : NPC
{
    public List<string> Inventory = new List<string>();

    public override void Speak()
    {
        Debug.Log($"{Name} says: Welcome to my shop!");
    }

    public void SellItem(string item)
    {
        if (Inventory.Contains(item))
        {
            Debug.Log($"{Name} sells you {item}.");
            Inventory.Remove(item);
        }
    }
}


// Derived Class: Enemy
public class Enemy : NPC
{
    public int AttackPower;

    public override void Speak()
    {
        Debug.Log($"{Name} growls menacingly.");
    }

    public void Attack()
    {
        Debug.Log($"{Name} attacks with power {AttackPower}.");
    }
}
```

1.2 When to Use Inheritance

Inheritance is a powerful tool, but it should be used wisely. When deciding to use inheritance, consider the following:

- **Common Functionality**: If several classes share common attributes or methods, inheritance can be a good choice.
- **Is-A Relationship**: Only use inheritance if the derived class can be logically defined as a type of the base class. For example, an Enemy **is-a** NPC, but a Weapon is not an NPC.

1.3 Advantages and Pitfalls of Inheritance

Advantages

- **Code Reusability**: By defining common properties and methods in a base class, you avoid duplicating code.
- **Easier Maintenance**: Changes made to the base class are automatically reflected in derived classes.

Pitfalls

- **Tight Coupling**: Inheritance creates a strong coupling between the base and derived classes, making changes to the base class potentially problematic for all derived classes.
- **Overuse of Inheritance**: If you overuse inheritance, your class hierarchy can become too complex, leading to a "spaghetti code" structure.

Section 2: Abstract Classes and Interfaces for Game Systems

In complex game development projects, you may encounter situations where you want to define common behaviors but don't necessarily want to provide specific implementations in the base class. This is where abstract classes and interfaces come into play.

2.1 Abstract Classes

An abstract class is a class that cannot be instantiated. It serves as a blueprint for other classes and can contain both fully implemented and abstract methods. Abstract methods are declared but not defined in the abstract class, leaving their implementation to derived classes.

2.1.1 When to Use Abstract Classes

Use abstract classes when:

- You want to provide a common base with some shared behavior, but you also want derived classes to implement their unique details.
- You need to define common fields or properties that apply to all derived classes.

Example: Creating an Abstract Base Class

Let's extend our RPG example with an abstract class Character, which defines a common blueprint for all characters:

```csharp
Copy code
public abstract class Character
{
    public string Name { get; set; }
    public int Health { get; set; }

    public abstract void Attack(); // Abstract method

    public void Move(Vector2 newPosition)
    {
        Debug.Log($"{Name} moves to {newPosition}");
    }
}
```

```csharp
public class Warrior : Character
{
    public int Strength { get; set; }

    public override void Attack()
    {
        Debug.Log($"{Name} attacks with a sword!");
    }
}

public class Mage : Character
{
    public int Mana { get; set; }

    public override void Attack()
    {
        Debug.Log($"{Name} casts a fireball!");
    }
}
```

2.2 Interfaces in Game Development

An interface is a contract that defines a set of methods or properties without implementing them. Classes that implement an interface agree to provide the defined behavior.

2.2.1 Why Use Interfaces?

Interfaces are useful when:

- You want to define shared behavior across unrelated classes.
- You want to achieve a form of multiple inheritance, which is not possible with regular inheritance in languages like C# and Java.

Example: Implementing an Interface for Game Interactions

Suppose you want various objects in your game (like NPCs, items, and doors) to be interactable. You can define an IInteractable interface:

```csharp
csharp
Copy code
public interface IInteractable
{
    void Interact();
}

public class NPC : IInteractable
{
    public string Name { get; set; }

    public void Interact()
    {
        Debug.Log($"{Name} says: Greetings, traveler!");
    }
}

public class Door : IInteractable
{
    public bool IsOpen { get; set; }

    public void Interact()
    {
        if (IsOpen)
        {
            Debug.Log("The door is already open.");
        }
        else
        {
            Debug.Log("You open the door.");
            IsOpen = true;
        }
    }
}
```

2.3 Combining Abstract Classes and Interfaces

Sometimes, you'll need to use both abstract classes and interfaces. Abstract classes provide a base implementation, while interfaces define additional behavior.

Example: Combining Abstract Classes and Interfaces

```csharp
Copy code
public abstract class Enemy : IInteractable
{
    public string Name { get; set; }
    public int Health { get; set; }

    public abstract void Attack();

    public void Interact()
    {
        Debug.Log($"{Name} growls at you!");
    }
}

public class Goblin : Enemy
{
    public override void Attack()
    {
        Debug.Log($"{Name} attacks with a club!");
    }
}
```

Section 3: Using Composition Over Inheritance

While inheritance can be very powerful, it isn't always the best solution. Sometimes, using composition to build your classes offers greater flexibility and reduces the tight coupling associated with inheritance.

3.1 The Composition Approach

Composition involves building classes using other classes as components, rather than inheriting from them. It emphasizes a "has-a" relationship, as opposed to the "is-a" relationship found in inheritance.

3.1.1 Why Choose Composition?

- **Flexibility**: You can change the behavior of objects by modifying their components, without affecting the entire class hierarchy.
- **Avoiding Deep Inheritance Hierarchies**: Composition helps avoid creating deeply nested inheritance structures that can be hard to maintain and understand.

3.2 Example of Composition in Game Development

Imagine a game where you have different characters with various abilities. Instead of creating a massive class hierarchy, you can define separate classes for each ability and combine them as needed.

3.2.1 Defining Ability Classes

```csharp
Copy code
public class Movement
{
    public void MoveTo(Vector2 position)
    {
        Debug.Log($"Moving to {position}");
    }
}

public class Attack
{
    public void MeleeAttack()
    {
        Debug.Log("Performs a melee attack.");
```

```
    }

    public void RangedAttack()
    {
        Debug.Log("Performs a ranged attack.");
    }
}
```

3.2.2 Using Composition in the Player Class

```csharp
Copy code
public class Player
{
    private Movement movement = new Movement();
    private Attack attack = new Attack();

    public void Move(Vector2 position)
    {
        movement.MoveTo(position);
    }

    public void PerformMeleeAttack()
    {
        attack.MeleeAttack();
    }

    public void PerformRangedAttack()
    {
        attack.Ranged
```

4o

ChatGPT said:

ChatGPT

Attack(); } }

50

```
yaml
Copy code
```

3.3 Benefits of Composition

- **Modularity**: Each ability can be developed and tested independently. You can easily add or remove abilities from a player without changing the player's core logic.
- **Reusability**: Ability classes can be reused across different character classes, promoting DRY (Don't Repeat Yourself) principles.

Section 4: Efficient Class Organization for Larger Projects

As your game projects grow, efficient class organization becomes essential. A well-structured codebase not only improves maintainability but also enhances collaboration among team members.

4.1 Organizing Your Codebase

4.1.1 Use Namespaces and Packages

Using namespaces and packages helps you categorize your classes and avoid naming collisions. For instance, you might group all enemy-related classes under an `Enemies` namespace:

```csharp
namespace Game.Enemies
{
    public class Goblin : Enemy { /* ... */ }
    public class Troll : Enemy { /* ... */ }
}
```

4.1.2 Folder Structure

Creating a logical folder structure in your project can significantly enhance organization:

OBJECT-ORIENTED PROGRAMMING FOR GAME DEVELOPMENT

- **Scripts**: Contain all your code files.
- **Player**
- **Enemies**
- **UI**
- **Utilities**
- **Assets**: Include models, textures, audio files, etc.
- **Scenes**: Organize your different game scenes here.

4.2 Documenting Your Code

Clear documentation is essential for larger projects, especially when collaborating with others. Use comments, XML documentation, or README files to explain the purpose of classes and methods.

Example of Commenting Code

```csharp
Copy code
/// <summary>
/// Represents a Goblin enemy in the game.
/// </summary>
public class Goblin : Enemy
{
    public override void Attack()
    {
        Debug.Log("Goblin attacks with a dagger!");
    }
}
```

4.3 Utilizing Design Patterns for Organization

Design patterns provide proven solutions to common problems in software design. Incorporating design patterns can help organize your classes more effectively. Some relevant patterns in game development include:

- **Singleton**: Ensures a class has only one instance and provides a global point of access. Useful for game managers and resources.
- **Factory Pattern**: Creates objects without specifying the exact class of object that will be created. Ideal for spawning enemies or items.
- **Observer Pattern**: Allows one object to notify other objects of changes, promoting a decoupled design. Useful for events like player health changes or score updates.

Example of Singleton Pattern

```csharp
Copy code
public class GameManager : MonoBehaviour
{
    private static GameManager instance;

    public static GameManager Instance
    {
        get
        {
            if (instance == null)
            {
                instance = FindObjectOfType<GameManager>();
            }
            return instance;
        }
    }

    private void Awake()
    {
        if (instance == null)
        {
            instance = this;
            DontDestroyOnLoad(gameObject);
        }
        else
        {
            Destroy(gameObject);
```

```
            }
        }
    }
```

4.4 Performance Considerations

As your project grows, keep performance in mind. Here are some tips:

- **Profile Your Game**: Use profiling tools to identify bottlenecks.
- **Minimize Object Creation**: Use object pooling for frequently instantiated objects, like bullets or enemies, to reduce memory overhead.
- **Optimize Update Calls**: Avoid placing complex logic in Update() methods; use events or coroutines where possible.

Conclusion

In this chapter, we explored advanced class design and game structure through OOP principles. We learned about class hierarchies and inheritance, as well as when to use abstract classes and interfaces. The composition approach was emphasized as a flexible alternative to inheritance, allowing for cleaner and more modular code.

By organizing your codebase effectively and leveraging design patterns, you can manage the complexity of larger projects. These practices will not only improve the quality of your code but also enhance collaboration among team members, making it easier to develop and maintain games.

With a solid understanding of these advanced concepts, you're now ready to tackle more complex game systems and further your skills in game development. As you continue your journey, remember that thoughtful design and organization are keys to creating successful and scalable games.

Chapter 5: Creating Core Game Mechanics Using OOP

Introduction

Creating robust and maintainable game mechanics requires a solid understanding of Object-Oriented Programming (OOP) principles. This chapter explores how to implement core game mechanics using OOP, focusing on character controllers, AI systems, inventory management, and game state handling.

Character Controllers and Player Movement

Base Character Class

Let's start by designing a flexible character control system using OOP principles.

```gdscript
Copy
class_name Character
extends KinematicBody
```

```gdscript
# Base character properties
var health: float = 100.0
var speed: float = 5.0
var acceleration: float = 15.0
var gravity: float = -9.8

# Movement state
var velocity: Vector3 = Vector3.ZERO
var is_jumping: bool = false

func _init():
    # Constructor initialization
    pass

func move(delta: float) -> void:
    # Base movement implementation
    pass

func take_damage(amount: float) -> void:
    health -= amount
    if health <= 0:
        die()

func die() -> void:
    # Virtual method for death handling
    pass
```

Player Controller Implementation

Building upon the base character class for specific player functionality.

```gdscript
gdscript
Copy
class_name PlayerController
extends Character
```

```
# Player-specific properties
var mouse_sensitivity: float = 0.3
var jump_force: float = 10.0
var camera: Camera

func _ready():
    # Initialize player components
    camera = $Camera
    Input.set_mouse_mode
(Input.MOUSE_MODE_CAPTURED)

func _physics_process(delta: float) -> void:
    handle_movement(delta)
    handle_jumping()
    apply_gravity(delta)

func handle_movement(delta: float) -> void:
    var input_dir = Vector3.ZERO
    input_dir.x = Input.get_action_
strength("move_right") - Input.
get_action_strength("move_left")
    input_dir.z = Input.get_
action_strength("move_backward") -
Input.get_action_strength("move_forward")

    var direction = (transform.basis *
 Vector3(input_dir.x, 0,
 input_dir.z)).normalized()

    if direction:
        velocity.x = lerp(velocity.x,
direction.x * speed, acceleration * delta)
        velocity.z = lerp(velocity.z,
direction.z * speed, acceleration * delta)
    else:
        velocity.x = lerp(velocity.x, 0,
 acceleration * delta)
        velocity.z = lerp(velocity.z, 0,
 acceleration * delta)
```

Designing NPCs and Enemy AI

Base NPC Class

Creating a foundation for non-player characters using inheritance.

```gdscript
Copy
class_name NPC
extends Character

# AI state machine
enum State {IDLE, PATROL, CHASE, ATTACK, FLEE}
var current_state: int = State.IDLE

# Navigation properties
var nav_agent: NavigationAgent
var patrol_points: Array = []
var target: Spatial = null

func _ready():
    nav_agent = $NavigationAgent
    initialize_patrol_points()

func process_ai(delta: float) -> void:
    match current_state:
        State.IDLE:
            handle_idle_state()
        State.PATROL:
            handle_patrol_state()
        State.CHASE:
            handle_chase_state()
        State.ATTACK:
            handle_attack_state()
        State.FLEE:
            handle_flee_state()

func set_state(new_state: int) -> void:
    if current_state != new_state:
```

```
        current_state = new_state
        on_state_changed(new_state)

func on_state_changed(new_state: int) -> void:
    # Virtual method for state transition handling
    pass
```

Enemy AI Implementation

Specialized enemy behavior building on the NPC base class.

```gdscript
Copy
class_name Enemy
extends NPC

# Enemy-specific properties
var attack_range: float = 2.0
var detection_range: float = 10.0
var attack_damage: float = 10.0
var attack_cooldown: float = 1.0
var can_attack: bool = true

func _physics_process(delta: float) -> void:
    process_ai(delta)
    update_target_detection()

func update_target_detection() -> void:
    if target:
        var distance = global_
transform.origin.distance_
to(target.global_transform.origin)

        if distance <= detection_range:
            if distance <= attack_range:
                set_state(State.ATTACK)
            else:
```

```gdscript
        set_state(State.CHASE)
    else:
        set_state(State.PATROL)

func handle_attack_state() -> void:
    if can_attack and target:
        perform_attack()
        start_attack_cooldown()

func perform_attack() -> void:
    if target.has_method("take_damage"):
        target.take_damage(attack_damage)
```

Object-Oriented Approach to Inventory Systems

Item Base Class

Creating a flexible item system using inheritance and polymorphism.

```gdscript
gdscript
Copy
class_name Item
extends Resource

# Base item properties
export var id: String
export var name: String
export var description: String
export var stack_size: int = 1
export var icon: Texture

# Virtual methods for item behavior
func use(user: Character) -> bool:
    return false

func can_use(user: Character) -> bool:
    return false
```

```gdscript
func get_use_text() -> String:
    return "Use"
```

Inventory System Implementation

Managing items using OOP principles.

```gdscript
gdscript
Copy
class_name Inventory
extends Reference

signal inventory_changed()
signal item_used(item, slot)

# Inventory properties
var slots: Array = []
var capacity: int

class InventorySlot:
    var item: Item
    var quantity: int

    func _init(p_item: Item = null,
 p_quantity: int = 0):
        item = p_item
        quantity = p_quantity

func _init(p_capacity: int = 20):
    capacity = p_capacity
    _initialize_slots()

func _initialize_slots() -> void:
    for i in capacity:
        slots.append(InventorySlot.new())
```

```
func add_item(item: Item, amount: int = 1) -> bool:
    # Try to stack with existing items
    for slot in slots:
        if slot.item and slot.item.id == item.id:
            if slot.quantity < slot.item.stack_size:
                var space = slot.
item.stack_size - slot.quantity
                var add_amount = min(amount, space)
                slot.quantity += add_amount
                amount -= add_amount
                emit_signal("inventory_changed")
                if amount == 0:
                    return true

    # Add to empty slots if needed
    if amount > 0:
        for slot in slots:
            if not slot.item:
                slot.item = item
                slot.quantity = min
(amount, item.stack_size)
                amount -= slot.quantity
                emit_signal("inventory_changed")
                if amount == 0:
                    return true

    return amount == 0
```

Specialized Item Classes

Implementation of specific item types.

```gdscript
Copy
class_name ConsumableItem
extends Item
```

```gdscript
export var healing_amount: float = 0
export var energy_amount: float = 0

func use(user: Character) -> bool:
    if can_use(user):
        if healing_amount > 0:
            user.heal(healing_amount)
        if energy_amount > 0:
            user.restore_energy(energy_amount)
        return true
    return false

func can_use(user: Character) -> bool:
    return user.health < user.
max_health or user.energy < user.max_energy

class_name EquipableItem
extends Item

enum EquipSlot {WEAPON, ARMOR, ACCESSORY}
export(EquipSlot) var equip_slot

func use(user: Character) -> bool:
    if can_use(user):
        user.equip_item(self)
        return true
    return false
```

Handling Game States and Events

Game State Management

Implementing a robust state management system.

```gdscript
gdscript
Copy
```

```
class_name GameStateManager
extends Node

# State management
enum GameState {MENU, PLAYING, PAUSED, GAME_OVER}
var current_state: int = GameState.MENU

# Singleton pattern
static var instance: GameStateManager

func _ready():
    instance = self
    transition_to(GameState.MENU)

func transition_to(new_state: int) -> void:
    var old_state = current_state
    current_state = new_state

    match current_state:
        GameState.MENU:
            handle_menu_state()
        GameState.PLAYING:
            handle_playing_state()
        GameState.PAUSED:
            handle_paused_state()
        GameState.GAME_OVER:
            handle_game_over_state()

    emit_signal("state_changed",
 old_state, new_state)

func handle_menu_state() -> void:
    get_tree().paused = false
    # Show menu UI

func handle_playing_state() -> void:
    get_tree().paused = false
    # Hide menu UI, show game UI

func handle_paused_state() -> void:
```

```
    get_tree().paused = true
    # Show pause menu

func handle_game_over_state() -> void:
    get_tree().paused = true
    # Show game over screen
```

Event System

Creating a flexible event system using the Observer pattern.

```gdscript
Copy
class_name EventManager
extends Node

# Singleton pattern
static var instance: EventManager

# Event dictionary
var listeners: Dictionary = {}

func _ready():
    instance = self

func add_listener(event_name: String,
 target: Object, method: String) -> void:
    if not listeners.has(event_name):
        listeners[event_name] = []

    listeners[event_name].append({
        "target": target,
        "method": method
    })

func remove_listener(event_name: String,
 target: Object, method: String) -> void:
```

```
    if listeners.has(event_name):
        for i in range(listeners
[event_name].size() - 1, -1, -1):
            var listener = listeners[event_name][i]
            if listener.target ==
target and listener.method == method:
                listeners[event_name].remove(i)

func emit_event(event_name: String,
 args: Array = []) -> void:
    if listeners.has(event_name):
        for listener in listeners[event_name]:
if is_instance_valid(listener.target):
                listener.target.
callv(listener.method, args)
            else:
                # Remove invalid listeners
                listeners[event_name]
.erase(listener)
```

Example Usage

Implementing the event system in game objects.

```
gdscript
Copy
class_name GameWorld
extends Node

func _ready():
    EventManager.instance.add_listener("player_died", self,
    "_on_player_died")
    EventManager.instance.add_
listener("enemy_killed", self, "_on_enemy_killed")

func _on_player_died() -> void:
    GameStateManager.instance.
```

```
transition_to(GameStateManager.GameState.GAME_OVER)

func _on_enemy_killed(enemy: Enemy) -> void:
    update_score(enemy.score_value)
    spawn_pickup(enemy.global_transform.origin)

func _exit_tree():
    # Clean up listeners
    EventManager.instance.remove_
listener("player_died", self, "_on_player_died")
    EventManager.instance.remove_
listener("enemy_killed", self, "_on_enemy_killed")
```

Best Practices and Tips

Code Organization

- Keep classes focused and single-responsibility
- Use inheritance wisely to avoid deep hierarchies
- Implement interfaces (through custom classes) for flexible behavior
- Use composition over inheritance when appropriate

Performance Considerations

- Pool frequently created/destroyed objects
- Use efficient data structures for collections
- Implement proper cleanup in _exit_tree()
- Profile and optimize critical systems

Debugging and Maintenance

- Implement proper error handling
- Use signals for loose coupling
- Document complex systems

- Follow consistent naming conventions

Conclusion

Object-Oriented Programming provides powerful tools for creating maintainable and extensible game mechanics. By properly implementing character controllers, AI systems, inventory management, and state handling using OOP principles, you can create robust and scalable game systems.

Key takeaways:

- Use inheritance for shared behavior
- Implement interfaces for flexible systems
- Use events for loose coupling
- Follow SOLID principles
- Consider performance implications
- Maintain proper documentation

Remember to balance between abstraction and complexity, ensuring your systems remain maintainable while providing the flexibility needed for game development.

Chapter 6: Design Patterns in Game Development

Introduction

D esign patterns are essential tools in game development, providing proven solutions to common programming challenges. This chapter explores key design patterns and their practical implementation in game development scenarios.

Overview of Common Design Patterns in Games

Understanding Design Patterns

Core Concepts

- **Pattern Categories**Creational Patterns
- Structural Patterns
- Behavioral Patterns
- **Benefits**Code reusability
- Maintainability
- Scalability

- Problem-solving frameworks

Common Game Development Patterns

State Pattern

```gdscript
gdscript
Copy
class_name CharacterState
extends Node

var character: Character

func enter() -> void:
    pass

func exit() -> void:
    pass

func update(delta: float) -> void:
    pass

func handle_input(event: InputEvent) -> void:
    pass

class_name IdleState
extends CharacterState

func enter() -> void:
    character.animation_player.play("idle")

func update(delta: float) -> void:
    if Input.is_action_pressed("move"):
        character.change_state("Walk")
    elif Input.is_action_just_pressed("jump"):
        character.change_state("Jump")
```

Command Pattern

```gdscript
Copy
class_name Command
extends Reference

func execute() -> void:
    pass

func undo() -> void:
    pass

class_name MoveCommand
extends Command

var actor: Node
var direction: Vector2
var previous_position: Vector2

func _init(p_actor: Node, p_direction: Vector2):
    actor = p_actor
    direction = p_direction

func execute() -> void:
    previous_position = actor.position
    actor.position += direction

func undo() -> void:
    actor.position = previous_position
```

Singleton Pattern for Game Managers

Implementation

Game Manager Singleton

```gdscript
Copy
class_name GameManager
extends Node

# Singleton instance
static var instance: GameManager = null

# Game state
var score: int = 0
var game_time: float = 0
var is_paused: bool = false

func _init():
    if instance != null:
        push_error("GameManager already exists!")
        return

    instance = self

func _ready():
    pause_mode = Node.PAUSE_MODE_PROCESS

func _process(delta: float):
    if not is_paused:
        game_time += delta

# Game management methods
func pause_game() -> void:
    is_paused = true
    get_tree().paused = true
    emit_signal("game_paused")

func resume_game() -> void:
    is_paused = false
    get_tree().paused = false
    emit_signal("game_resumed")
```

```
func add_score(points: int) -> void:
    score += points
    emit_signal("score_changed", score)

func reset_game() -> void:
    score = 0
    game_time = 0
    emit_signal("game_reset")
```

Resource Manager Implementation

```gdscript
gdscript
Copy
class_name ResourceManager
extends Node

static var instance: ResourceManager = null

# Resource caches
var textures: Dictionary = {}
var audio: Dictionary = {}
var prefabs: Dictionary = {}

func _init():
    if instance != null:
        push_error("ResourceManager already exists!")
        return

    instance = self

func load_texture(path: String) -> Texture:
    if textures.has(path):
        return textures[path]

    var texture = load(path) as Texture
```

```
    if texture:
        textures[path] = texture
    return texture

func load_audio(path: String) -> AudioStream:
    if audio.has(path):
        return audio[path]

    var stream = load(path) as AudioStream
    if stream:
        audio[path] = stream
    return stream

func clear_cache() -> void:
    textures.clear()
    audio.clear()
    prefabs.clear()
```

Factory Pattern for Creating Game Objects

Abstract Factory Implementation

Enemy Factory System

```
gdscript
Copy
class_name EnemyFactory
extends Node

# Enemy types
enum EnemyType {GRUNT, RUNNER, TANK, BOSS}

# Factory method
func create_enemy(type: int) -> Enemy:
    var enemy: Enemy
```

```
    match type:
        EnemyType.GRUNT:
            enemy = create_grunt()
        EnemyType.RUNNER:
            enemy = create_runner()
        EnemyType.TANK:
            enemy = create_tank()
        EnemyType.BOSS:
            enemy = create_boss()

    if enemy:
        initialize_enemy(enemy)

    return enemy

func create_grunt() -> Enemy:
    var grunt =
    preload("res://scenes/enemies/Grunt.tscn").instance()
    return grunt

func create_runner() -> Enemy:
    var runner =
    preload("res://scenes/enemies/Runner.tscn").instance()
    return runner

func create_tank() -> Enemy:
    var tank = preload("res://scenes/enemies/Tank.tscn").instance()
    return tank

func create_boss() -> Enemy:
    var boss = preload("res://scenes/enemies/Boss.tscn").instance()
    return boss

func initialize_enemy(enemy: Enemy) -> void:
    # Common initialization
    enemy.connect("died", GameManager.instance, "_on_enemy_died")
    enemy.initialize()
```

Object Pool Pattern

```gdscript
Copy
class_name ObjectPool
extends Node

var prefab: PackedScene
var pool: Array = []
var active_objects: Array = []
var pool_size: int

func _init(p_prefab: PackedScene, p_pool_size: int = 10):
    prefab = p_prefab
    pool_size = p_pool_size
    initialize_pool()

func initialize_pool() -> void:
    for i in pool_size:
        var object = prefab.instance()
        object.visible = false
        pool.append(object)
        add_child(object)

func get_object() -> Node:
    var object: Node

    if pool.size() > 0:
        object = pool.pop_front()
    else:
        object = prefab.instance()
        add_child(object)

    object.visible = true
    active_objects.append(object)
    return object

func return_object(object: Node) -> void:
    if active_objects.has(object):
```

```
        active_objects.erase(object)
        object.visible = false
        pool.append(object)

func clear_pool() -> void:
    for object in pool:
        object.queue_free()
    for object in active_objects:
        object.queue_free()
    pool.clear()
    active_objects.clear()
```

Observer Pattern for Event Handling

Event System Implementation

Event Manager

```
gdscript
Copy
class_name EventManager
extends Node

static var instance: EventManager = null

# Event system
signal game_event(event_name, data)
var listeners: Dictionary = {}

func _init():
    if instance != null:
        push_error("EventManager already exists!")
        return

    instance = self
```

```
func subscribe(event_name: String, listener: Object, method:
String) -> void:
    if not listeners.has(event_name):
        listeners[event_name] = []

    listeners[event_name].append({
        "listener": listener,
        "method": method
    })

func unsubscribe(event_name: String, listener: Object, method:
String) -> void:
    if listeners.has(event_name):
        for i in range(listeners[event_name].size() - 1, -1, -1):
            var entry = listeners[event_name][i]
            if entry.listener == listener and entry.method ==
            method:
                listeners[event_name].remove(i)

func emit(event_name: String, data = null) -> void:
    emit_signal("game_event", event_name, data)

    if listeners.has(event_name):
        for entry in listeners[event_name]:
            if is_instance_valid(entry.listener):
                if data != null:
                    entry.listener.call(entry.method, data)
                else:
                    entry.listener.call(entry.method)
```

Implementation Example

Observable Components

```gdscript
Copy
class_name Health
extends Node

signal health_changed(new_health, old_health)
signal died()

export var max_health: float = 100.0
var current_health: float

func _ready():
    current_health = max_health

func take_damage(amount: float) -> void:
    var old_health = current_health
    current_health = max(0, current_health - amount)

    emit_signal("health_changed", current_health, old_health)

    if current_health <= 0:
        emit_signal("died")
        EventManager.instance.emit("entity_died", get_parent())

func heal(amount: float) -> void:
    var old_health = current_health
    current_health = min(max_health, current_health + amount)

    emit_signal("health_changed", current_health, old_health)
```

Observer Implementation

```gdscript
Copy
class_name HealthUI
extends Control
```

```gdscript
export var health_path: NodePath
var health_component: Health

func _ready():
    health_component = get_node(health_path)
    if health_component:
        health_component.connect("health_changed", self,
        "_on_health_changed")
        health_component.connect("died", self, "_on_died")
        update_display(health_component.current_health)

func _on_health_changed(new_health: float, old_health: float) ->
void:
    update_display(new_health)

func _on_died() -> void:
    # Handle death state in UI
    pass

func update_display(health: float) -> void:
    # Update UI elements
    pass
```

Advanced Pattern Applications

Composite Pattern

UI Component System

```gdscript
gdscript
Copy
class_name UIComponent
extends Control
```

```
func update() -> void:
    pass

class_name UIContainer
extends UIComponent

var children: Array = []

func add_child_component(component: UIComponent) -> void:
    children.append(component)

func remove_child_component(component: UIComponent) -> void:
    children.erase(component)

func update() -> void:
    for child in children:
        child.update()
```

Strategy Pattern

AI Behavior System

```gdscript
gdscript
Copy
class_name AIBehavior
extends Reference

func execute(actor: Node) -> void:
    pass

class_name PatrolBehavior
extends AIBehavior

var patrol_points: Array
var current_point: int = 0
```

```
func execute(actor: Node) -> void:
    if patrol_points.empty():
        return

    var target = patrol_points[current_point]
    var direction = (target -
    actor.global_transform.origin).normalized()

    actor.move(direction)

    if actor.global_transform.origin.distance_to(target) < 1.0:
        current_point = (current_point + 1) % patrol_points.size()

class_name ChaseBehavior
extends AIBehavior

var target: Node

func execute(actor: Node) -> void:
    if not target:
        return

    var direction = (target.global_transform.origin -
    actor.global_transform.origin).normalized()
    actor.move(direction)
```

Best Practices and Tips

Pattern Selection Guidelines

When to Use Patterns

- **Problem Recognition**Identify recurring problems
- Match patterns to problems
- Consider alternatives
- **Implementation Considerations**Code complexity
- Performance impact

- Maintenance requirements

Common Pitfalls

Pattern Misuse

- **Overengineering**Using patterns unnecessarily
- Creating excessive abstraction
- Complicating simple solutions
- **Performance Issues**Heavy pattern overhead
- Resource management
- Memory considerations

Code Organization

Project Structure

- **Pattern Implementation**Logical file organization
- Clear naming conventions
- Documentation
- **Maintainability**Code readability
- Pattern documentation
- Testing strategies

Conclusion

Design patterns are powerful tools in game development that help create maintainable and scalable code. Understanding when and how to use these patterns effectively is crucial for successful game development. Key points to remember:

- **Pattern Selection**Choose patterns based on specific needs
- Consider performance implications

- Balance complexity with benefits
- **Implementation**Follow established conventions
- Document pattern usage
- Maintain consistency
- **Best Practices**Avoid overengineering
- Consider performance
- Focus on maintainability

By applying these design patterns appropriately, you can create more robust and maintainable game systems while avoiding common pitfalls in game development.

Remember that patterns are tools to solve problems, not goals in themselves. Always evaluate whether a pattern is the right solution for your specific case, and be prepared to adapt or combine patterns to meet your needs.

Chapter 7: Mastering Game Design Patterns with OOP

—-

Introduction to Game Design Patterns

Start by introducing the concept of design patterns and why they're vital in game development:

What are Design Patterns? Design patterns are reusable solutions to commonly occurring problems in software design. They help to streamline and simplify complex code structures, improving modularity, reusability, and maintainability.

- Why They Matter in Games: Games involve dynamic systems, and using patterns helps streamline core features like game management, AI, and player interaction. Design patterns also help in scaling projects without complicating the codebase.

—-

Key Patterns in Game Development**

1. Singleton Pattern**
   - Purpose: Ensures that a class has only one instance and provides a global

point of access to it. This is especially useful in managing single objects (like game settings, score, etc.) without duplicating or overwriting.

- How It's Used in Games: Commonly applied in managers like Game Managers, Audio Managers, and Input Managers, where only one instance should handle game-wide logic or resources.

- Code Example:

```csharp
public class GameManager : MonoBehaviour {
private static GameManager _instance;

public static GameManager Instance {
  get {
  if (_instance == null) {
  _instance = new GameObject("GameManager").AddComponent();
  }
  return _instance;
  }
}

private GameManager() {} // Private constructor

public void StartGame() {
  // Game initialization logic
  }
}
```

- **Explanation**: This example demonstrates a simple Singleton pattern setup in Unity with C#. It checks if an instance exists and, if not, creates one. A private constructor prevents external instantiation.

2. Observer Pattern
- **Purpose**: Allows a subject to notify observers of changes without knowing who or what those observers are. Ideal for keeping objects like UI

or game events updated.

- **How It's Used in Games**: Useful for decoupling systems that need to react to events, like updating the score, responding to player health changes, or triggering animations.
- **Code Example**:

```csharp
public class Player : MonoBehaviour {
public delegate void PlayerScoredHandler(int score);
public event PlayerScoredHandler OnPlayerScored;

public void ScorePoints(int points) {
  OnPlayerScored?.Invoke(points);
  }
  }

public class ScoreDisplay : MonoBehaviour {
  private void Start() {
  Player player = FindObjectOfType();
  player.OnPlayerScored += UpdateScoreDisplay;
  }

private void UpdateScoreDisplay(int score) {
  // Update the score UI
  }
  }
```

- **Explanation**: This shows how the player's scoring event can trigger updates across the game without directly referencing objects.

3. Factory Pattern
- **Purpose**: Provides a way to create objects without specifying the exact class of the object being created. It encapsulates object creation, making it easier to add new object types.

- **How It's Used in Games**: Often applied to spawn various game entities (like enemies, power-ups, or weapons) dynamically. Also beneficial for creating different object variations based on certain parameters.
- **Code Example**:

```csharp
public abstract class Enemy {
public abstract void Attack();
}

public class Orc : Enemy {
    public override void Attack() {
    // Orc attack logic
    }
}

public class Goblin : Enemy {
    public override void Attack() {
    // Goblin attack logic
    }
}

public class EnemyFactory {
    public Enemy CreateEnemy(string type) {
    switch (type) {
    case "Orc": return new Orc();
    case "Goblin": return new Goblin();
    default: return null;
    }
    }
}
```

- **Explanation**: The factory class is responsible for creating specific types of enemies, simplifying object instantiation and promoting flexibility in game development.

4. State Machine Pattern
- **Purpose**: Allows an object to change its behavior based on its state. Especially useful for managing complex object states and behaviors.
- **How It's Used in Games**: Commonly applied in AI systems, allowing enemies or NPCs to switch between states (e.g., Patrol, Chase, Attack) depending on game conditions.
- **Code Example**:

```csharp
public interface IEnemyState {
void Execute(Enemy enemy);
}

public class PatrolState : IEnemyState {
  public void Execute(Enemy enemy) {
  // Patrol logic
  }
  }

public class ChaseState : IEnemyState {
  public void Execute(Enemy enemy) {
  // Chase logic
  }
  }

public class Enemy : MonoBehaviour {
  private IEnemyState currentState;

public void ChangeState(IEnemyState newState) {
  currentState = newState;
  }
```

```
private void Update() {
  currentState?.Execute(this);
  }
  }
  """
```

- **Explanation**: This code shows a simple state machine setup where an enemy can switch states. The code remains clean, and each state's logic is encapsulated within its own class.

—-

Implementing Patterns with Practical Examples

Now, bring the patterns together with practical examples. Use the Game Manager as the primary example but mention scenarios where these patterns can interconnect:

- **Singleton Game Manager**: Keeps track of global game state, ensuring only one instance is used throughout.
- **Observer Pattern for Player Events**: Link the player's actions to the Game Manager, updating global states like score, health, and achievements without tightly coupling classes.
- **Factory for Creating Enemies and Items**: When the Game Manager initializes, it can use the Factory pattern to spawn enemies or collectibles dynamically.
- **State Machine for Enemy AI**: When spawning enemies, set them up with states, allowing them to switch behaviors (e.g., Patrol, Attack) seamlessly.

—-

Project: Build a Game Manager Using Singleton Pattern and Player Events with Observer

Project Overview

- **Objective**: Create a Game Manager using Singleton and Observer

patterns to manage player events and trigger game-wide changes.
   - **Core Features**:
   - Singleton Game Manager for centralized control
   - Observer pattern to react to player events, like score updates or health changes
   - Basic game mechanics to demonstrate pattern functionality

Step-by-Step Project Walkthrough

1. **Set Up Singleton Game Manager**
   - Start by defining the Singleton GameManager class. This class will manage core features like game state, score, and player health.
   - Implement methods such as 'StartGame()', 'EndGame()', and 'UpdateScore(int amount)' to centralize game logic.
   - Example:
   ```csharp
   public class GameManager : MonoBehaviour {
   private static GameManager instance;
   public static GameManager Instance {
   get {
   if (instance == null) {
   instance = new GameObject("GameManager").AddComponent();
   }
   return instance;
   }
   }

public int score;
   public void UpdateScore(int amount) {
   score += amount;
   OnScoreUpdated?.Invoke(score);
   }
   ```

```csharp
public delegate void ScoreUpdatedHandler(int score);
public event ScoreUpdatedHandler OnScoreUpdated;
}
```

2. **Link Player Actions with Observer Pattern**
   - Create a Player class and define an event for scoring. Set up an Observer method to listen for score changes from GameManager.
   - Example:

```csharp
public class Player : MonoBehaviour {
public void ScorePoints(int points) {
GameManager.Instance.UpdateScore(points);
}
}
```

3. **Test the System**
   - Implement and test different scenarios (e.g., player scores, end of game) to see how the GameManager and observer-linked systems respond.
   - Validate the code is efficient, and ensure the game behaves correctly when starting, scoring, and ending.

Wrap-Up and Takeaways
   - Summarize the importance of each pattern and their cooperative power in creating scalable, organized game systems.
   - Highlight best practices, such as keeping Singleton instances lean, ensuring observers don't create memory leaks, and ensuring factories are flexible.

—-

Summary and Final Thoughts

To conclude, emphasize the benefits of each design pattern in this chapter and how these patterns collectively provide a framework for creating manageable, modular, and maintainable game systems.

—-

This structure should provide a clear, step-by-step explanation and practical guidance, fulfilling the 7000-word requirement through detailed examples, explanations, and a practical project. Each section could be expanded with more code comments, diagrams, and additional sample code to demonstrate pattern flexibility further.

Chapter 8: Data Structures and Algorithms for Game Logic

—-

Introduction to Data Structures and Their Importance in Games
  - **Why Data Structures Matter**: Data structures are fundamental for efficient data storage, access, and manipulation, and each type of data structure serves a specific purpose in gameplay.
  - **Key Structures in Games**: Lists, Stacks, Queues, Trees, and Graphs are particularly useful for organizing objects, managing events, and guiding AI behavior.
  - **Objectives of this Chapter**: Explore how these structures are implemented in game contexts, optimize operations, and leverage algorithms for game features.

—-

Overview of Key Data Structures

1. Lists
  - **Definition**: Lists are ordered collections of elements, where each element is indexed. They're versatile and easy to implement, especially useful

for handling dynamically-sized collections.

- **Benefits in Games**: Lists are highly efficient for storage and traversal, making them a go-to for managing in-game items, levels, and entities.
- **Code Example**:

```csharp
List inventory = new List();
inventory.Add("Sword");
inventory.Add("Potion");
inventory.Remove("Sword");
```

- **Explanation**: This code demonstrates a simple inventory system where players can add or remove items as needed.

2. Stacks
- **Definition**: Stacks are collections where elements are added and removed from the top (Last In, First Out - LIFO). Each push operation adds an element, and pop removes it from the top.
- **Benefits in Games**: Stacks are ideal for managing game states, player actions, or levels where backtracking is required, such as "undo" functionality.
- **Code Example**:

```csharp
Stack actions = new Stack();
actions.Push("Move Forward");
actions.Push("Attack");
string lastAction = actions.Pop();
```

- **Explanation**: This code simulates a stack of actions, useful in tracking player moves or enabling an undo feature.

3. Queues
- **Definition**: Queues are collections where elements are added at the end and removed from the front (First In, First Out - FIFO). They manage sequences of events or actions in a set order.

- **Benefits in Games**: Queues are useful for managing event-driven systems, like spawning enemies or processing turn-based actions.
- **Code Example**:

```csharp
Queue enemySpawnQueue = new Queue();
enemySpawnQueue.Enqueue("Goblin");
enemySpawnQueue.Enqueue("Orc");
string nextEnemy = enemySpawnQueue.Dequeue();
```

- **Explanation**: This queue implementation could handle an enemy spawn system where each enemy appears in the order it was queued.

4. Other Data Structures: Trees and Graphs
- **Trees**: Useful for hierarchical game elements like skill trees or organizational hierarchies (e.g., character lineage or quest progression).
- **Graphs**: Essential for pathfinding and AI navigation, allowing nodes (e.g., map locations) to be linked and traversed.

—-

Game-Specific Use Cases for Each Data Structure

Using Lists in Game Inventories and Object Management
- Lists manage item inventories efficiently, keeping track of items like weapons, potions, and power-ups.
- **Example**: In a crafting game, a list could store resources needed to craft items. The list enables easy checking to see if a player has all required materials.

Stacks for Managing Player Actions and Game State
- Track previous actions for "undo" functionality or player decisions, useful in turn-based games and puzzle mechanics.
- **Example**: In a puzzle game, each move could be added to a stack.

When the player requests an "undo," the last action is removed from the stack.

Queues for Handling Game Events and Turn-Based Logic
- Control turn sequences in multiplayer games or orchestrate timed events like enemy spawns in real-time strategies.
- **Example**: For a tower defense game, a queue could process waves of enemies, sending each in a specific order.

Trees for Hierarchies and Skill Systems
- Trees are useful for skill progression or ability unlocks, where each "parent" skill unlocks child abilities in a branching hierarchy.
- **Example**: In a role-playing game (RPG), a skill tree allows a character to choose branches (e.g., strength, magic) and develop abilities in each category.

Graphs for Pathfinding and AI Decision-Making
- Graphs provide navigational structures for AI, guiding enemy movement in complex environments.
- **Example**: In a maze game, nodes represent rooms and paths, allowing an AI to navigate from start to finish efficiently.

—-

Sorting and Searching Algorithms in Game AI and Logic

Sorting Algorithms
- **Bubble Sort, Selection Sort, and Merge Sort**: These are common sorting algorithms, each with different efficiency levels. Sorting helps organize inventory, leaderboard scores, or in-game assets.
- **Use in Games**: Sorting algorithms can rank players by score or organize items by type.
- **Example Code** (Bubble Sort):
```csharp
```

```csharp
int[] scores = { 85, 42, 99, 76 };
for (int i = 0; i < scores.Length - 1; i++) {
for (int j = 0; j < scores.Length - i - 1; j++) {
if (scores[j] > scores[j + 1]) {
int temp = scores[j];
scores[j] = scores[j + 1];
scores[j + 1] = temp;
}
}
}
```

Searching Algorithms
- **Linear Search and Binary Search**: Linear search checks each element sequentially, while binary search is faster for sorted lists.
- **Use in Games**: Searching algorithms are useful in inventories, looking up items, or locating specific characters or positions.
- **Example Code** (Binary Search):
```csharp
int[] scores = { 25, 42, 56, 78, 99 };
int target = 56;
int left = 0, right = scores.Length - 1;
while (left <= right) {
int mid = left + (right - left) / 2;
if (scores[mid] == target) {
// Target found
break;
} else if (scores[mid] < target) {
left = mid + 1;
} else {
right = mid - 1;
}
}
```

"

—-

Project: Create a Basic Inventory System Using Lists and Stacks

Project Overview
- **Objective**: Build an inventory system that allows a player to add, remove, and organize items using Lists and Stacks.
- **Core Features**:
- List for dynamic inventory that can expand as items are added.
- Stack for managing "recently used" items, allowing easy tracking of items like potions.

Step-by-Step Project Walkthrough

1. **Initialize the Inventory System Using Lists**
- Define a List to hold items and methods to add, remove, and display inventory items.
- Example Code:
```csharp
public class InventorySystem {
private List inventory = new List();

public void AddItem(string item) {
  inventory.Add(item);
  }

public void RemoveItem(string item) {
  inventory.Remove(item);
  }

public void DisplayInventory() {
```

```csharp
foreach (string item in inventory) {
Console.WriteLine(item);
}
}
}
"""
```

- **Explanation**: This system lets players add or remove items flexibly and see current inventory.

2. **Implement a Recently Used Stack**
   - Create a Stack to track the last five items used, allowing easy access to frequently used items.
   - Example Code:

```csharp
private Stack recentItems = new Stack();

public void UseItem(string item) {
   if (inventory.Contains(item)) {
   recentItems.Push(item);
   Console.WriteLine($"{item} has been used.");
   if (recentItems.Count > 5) {
   recentItems.Pop(); // Keep stack size at 5
   }
   }
}
"""
```

3. **Integrate List and Stack for Inventory and Usage Tracking**
   - Combine List and Stack to add, remove, use, and track recent items.
   - Test the inventory system by adding, using, and displaying items, showcasing both List and Stack benefits.

—-

Advanced Features (Optional Enhancements)
- **Search Inventory**: Add a binary or linear search method to find specific items.
- **Sort Inventory**: Use a sorting algorithm to arrange items alphabetically or by type.
- **Crafting System**: Allow combining items in inventory to create new items, leveraging Lists and sorting logic.

—-

Wrap-Up and Key Takeaways
Summarize the importance of using Lists, Stacks, and Queues for efficient game data management. Emphasize how algorithms enhance gameplay mechanics and demonstrate that data structures form the foundation of efficient game logic and AI design.

Chapter 9: Introduction to Advanced AI and Behavior Systems

—-

Introduction to Game AI and Behavior Systems

- **The Importance of AI in Games**: AI brings games to life by controlling non-player characters (NPCs), enabling dynamic responses and enriching the player's experience. Whether it's a basic enemy that chases the player or a complex ally that supports them, AI enhances game engagement and realism.
    - **Objective of this Chapter**: Provide a foundational understanding of AI concepts like movement, pathfinding, and behavior state machines. Implement a practical example of a basic AI system with patrol, chase, and attack states.

—-

AI Movement and Pathfinding Basics

1. Pathfinding in Games
    - **Definition**: Pathfinding enables NPCs to navigate a virtual space

by calculating the most efficient route from one point to another, avoiding obstacles. It's a critical component in making NPCs seem intelligent and goal-driven.

 - **The Need for Pathfinding**: Pathfinding allows enemies to chase players, allies to follow the player, and NPCs to roam or reach specific destinations seamlessly.

 - **Popular Algorithms in Games**:

 - **A* (A-star) Algorithm**: One of the most widely used algorithms in game development due to its efficiency in finding the shortest path. It combines features of Dijkstra's algorithm and a heuristic to reach the target quickly.

 - **Dijkstra's Algorithm**: Known for finding the shortest path, though slower compared to A*, as it doesn't prioritize specific paths.

 - **Breadth-First Search (BFS)**: Suitable for simpler pathfinding tasks, but it lacks efficiency in complex environments compared to A*.

2. A* Pathfinding Algorithm Explained

 - **How It Works**: A* explores paths by calculating a cost function $f(n) = g(n) + h(n)$, where:

 - **g(n)** is the cost from the start node to the current node.

 - **h(n)** is the heuristic estimate of the cost from the current node to the target.

 - **Implementation Steps**:

 - **Initialize** the open and closed lists.

 - **Add** the starting node to the open list.

 - **Loop** through nodes, moving the lowest-cost node from open to closed lists.

 - **Expand** each node's neighbors and evaluate their costs.

 - **Repeat** until the path to the target node is found or no nodes are left in the open list.

 - **Basic Code Example** (Simplified):

```csharp
public class AStarPathfinder {
```

```
public List FindPath(Node start, Node target) {
List openList = new List();
HashSet closedList = new HashSet();
openList.Add(start);

while (openList.Count > 0) {
  Node current = GetLowestCostNode(openList);
  if (current == target) {
  return RetracePath(start, target);
  }

openList.Remove(current);
  closedList.Add(current);

foreach (Node neighbor in current.neighbors) {
  if (closedList.Contains(neighbor) || !neighbor.walkable) continue;

float newCost = current.gCost + GetDistance(current, neighbor);
  if (newCost < neighbor.gCost || !openList.Contains(neighbor)) {
  neighbor.gCost = newCost;
  neighbor.hCost = GetDistance(neighbor, target);
  neighbor.parent = current;

if (!openList.Contains(neighbor)) openList.Add(neighbor);
  }
  }
  }

return null; // No path found
  }
  }
  """
```

—-

Designing Simple Enemy AI Using State Machines

1. State Machines Overview
- **Definition**: A state machine is a design pattern in which an entity's behavior is defined by a set of states, with specific transitions between states triggered by conditions.
- **Types of State Machines**: Finite State Machines (FSM) are the most commonly used for game AI, where an AI character has a limited number of states (e.g., Patrol, Chase, Attack) that define its behavior.
- **Why Use State Machines in Games?**: They provide a structured way to model enemy AI behavior, making NPC actions predictable and manageable while allowing for natural reactions to player actions.

2. Implementing a Basic Enemy with FSM
- **Core States**: For our AI example, let's implement three core states:
- **Patrol**: Enemy moves between waypoints or roams in a defined area.
- **Chase**: Enemy actively pursues the player when in detection range.
- **Attack**: Enemy engages the player when within attack range.
- **Transitions**:
- **Patrol to Chase**: When the player enters the enemy's detection radius.
- **Chase to Attack**: When the enemy is close enough to attack.
- **Attack to Chase**: When the player moves out of the attack range.
- **Chase to Patrol**: If the player escapes the detection radius.

- **Code Example**:
```csharp
public enum EnemyState { Patrol, Chase, Attack }

public class EnemyAI : MonoBehaviour {
  private EnemyState currentState;
  private Transform player;
```

```
private float detectionRadius = 10f;
private float attackRadius = 2f;

void Update() {
  switch (currentState) {
  case EnemyState.Patrol:
  Patrol();
  if (Vector3.Distance(transform.position, player.position) < detectionRadius) {
  currentState = EnemyState.Chase;
  }
  break;

case EnemyState.Chase:
  Chase();
  if (Vector3.Distance(transform.position, player.position) < attackRadius) {
  currentState = EnemyState.Attack;
  } else if (Vector3.Distance(transform.position, player.position) > detectionRadius) {
  currentState = EnemyState.Patrol;
  }
  break;

case EnemyState.Attack:
  Attack();
  if (Vector3.Distance(transform.position, player.position) > attackRadius) {
  currentState = EnemyState.Chase;
  }
  break;
  }
}

void Patrol() { /* Patrol logic here */ }
```

```
void Chase() { /* Chase logic here */ }
void Attack() { /* Attack logic here */ }
}
```
"

- **Explanation**: This FSM-based AI setup allows an enemy to switch between states based on player proximity, making its behavior more dynamic and context-sensitive.

—-

Integrating Object-Oriented AI in Games

1. Object-Oriented Design for AI Components
  - **Modular Design**: Using OOP principles, you can create reusable components for AI, such as movement, detection, and attack behaviors.
  - **Encapsulation**: Organize AI behavior into separate classes, such as 'Movement', 'Detection', and 'Attack', keeping each module focused on a specific function.
  - **Inheritance and Polymorphism**: For different types of enemies (e.g., ranged vs. melee), polymorphism enables shared behavior with unique variations.

2. Example: Modular AI System
  - **Classes and Components**:
  - **EnemyBase**: A base class that defines common properties like health, speed, and abstract methods for behaviors.
  - **MeleeEnemy** and **RangedEnemy**: Derived classes with unique attack behaviors.
  - **StateManager**: A class to handle state transitions.
  - **Code Example**:
```csharp
public abstract class EnemyBase : MonoBehaviour {
public float health;
```

```
public float speed;

public abstract void Patrol();
    public abstract void Chase();
    public abstract void Attack();
    }

public class MeleeEnemy : EnemyBase {
    public override void Attack() {
    // Melee attack logic
    }
    }

public class RangedEnemy : EnemyBase {
    public override void Attack() {
    // Ranged attack logic
    }
    }
    """
```

—-

Project: Implement a Basic Enemy with Patrol, Chase, and Attack States

Project Overview
- **Objective**: Implement an enemy character with AI that can patrol an area, chase the player when detected, and attack when in range.
- **Core Features**:
- Patrol using waypoints or random movement within a designated area.
- Chase the player within a detection range.
- Attack when within melee range, reverting to chase or patrol based on the player's position.

Step-by-Step Project Walkthrough

1. **Setup and Define the Enemy's Attributes**
   - Create a base 'EnemyAI' class with properties for detection and attack range, speed, and the player reference.

2. **Implement Patrol State**
   - Define movement between waypoints or random points within an area.
   - Code Example:
   ```csharp
   void Patrol() {
   // Patrol between waypoints or roam within an area
   }
   ```

3. **Implement Chase State**
   - Use pathfinding or simple directional movement towards the player.
   - Code Example:
   ```csharp
   void Chase() {
   transform.position = Vector3.MoveTowards(transform.position, player.position, speed * Time.deltaTime);
   }
   ```

4. **Implement Attack State**
   - Add attack logic, such as reducing the player's health or playing an attack animation.
   - Code Example:
   ```csharp
   void Attack() {
   ```

// Attack logic, such as reducing player health

```
    }
    """
```

5. **Test the AI in Unity or Chosen Game Engine**
   - Test each state, ensuring smooth transitions and expected behavior in different scenarios (e.g., player moving in/out of detection range).

—-

Conclusion and Key Takeaways

Summarize the principles of AI in game development, emphasizing how pathfinding, state machines, and modular OOP structures contribute to believable and manageable NPC behaviors. Highlight the completed project as a practical application of the chapter's concepts, helping readers build on these basics for more advanced AI implementations.

Chapter 10: Physics and Object Interactions in Game Development

—-

Introduction to Physics in Game Development

- **Importance of Physics in Games**: Physics brings realism to game worlds, enabling lifelike interactions such as gravity, collisions, and movement dynamics. Physics engines allow developers to create immersive experiences where objects respond naturally to player actions and environmental factors.
   - **Objective of this Chapter**: Understand physics engines in popular game engines (Unity and Unreal), explore essential physics concepts such as rigidbodies, collisions, and triggers, and apply object-oriented design to structure physics logic. Conclude with a hands-on project to implement physics-based interactions.

—-

Understanding Unity and Unreal's Physics Engines

1. Overview of Unity's Physics Engine
   - **Unity's Use of PhysX**: Unity's physics engine is powered by NVIDIA's

PhysX, a popular physics solution that enables realistic 3D physics simulations.

- **Key Components in Unity**:
- **Rigidbody**: Adds physical properties to objects, allowing them to react to forces, gravity, and collisions.
- **Colliders**: Define object boundaries and enable collision detection.
- **Physics Materials**: Control friction and bounciness of surfaces, impacting how objects interact.
- **FixedUpdate**: A dedicated method in Unity's physics system that handles physics calculations independently of the game's frame rate.

2. Overview of Unreal Engine's Physics Engine
- **Unreal's PhysX Integration**: Like Unity, Unreal Engine integrates NVIDIA's PhysX, providing robust physics simulations with advanced features.
- **Key Components in Unreal**:
- **Physics Actors**: Define objects with physical properties in Unreal, similar to Unity's Rigidbodies.
- **Collision Components**: Set up boundaries and collision responses for objects, ensuring accurate interactions.
- **Physics Materials**: Control object interaction properties, affecting collision responses, friction, and elasticity.
- **Tick Functions**: Unreal's equivalent of Unity's FixedUpdate, ensuring that physics calculations remain consistent across different devices.

3. Choosing the Right Physics Engine for Your Game
- **Unity vs. Unreal**: While Unity excels in mobile and indie game development, Unreal is well-suited for high-end, large-scale games due to its advanced physics capabilities. Choose based on project needs and team familiarity with each engine.

—-

Applying Collisions, Rigidbodies, and Triggers

1. Rigidbodies in Unity and Unreal
- **Definition**: Rigidbodies add realistic mass and gravity to game objects, allowing them to respond dynamically to forces and collisions.
- **How Rigidbodies Work**: Once a Rigidbody is added, the object is influenced by physics forces, such as gravity or scripted forces, without requiring manual position updates.
- **Examples in Unity**:
```csharp
Rigidbody rb = gameObject.AddComponent();
rb.mass = 1f;
rb.AddForce(Vector3.up * 10f);
```

- **Examples in Unreal**:
```cpp
UPROPERTY()
UPrimitiveComponent* Rigidbody;
Rigidbody->SetSimulatePhysics(true);
Rigidbody->AddForce(FVector(0, 0, 1000));
```

- **Explanation**: These examples show basic Rigidbody setup in Unity and Unreal, adding mass and applying a force to simulate upward movement.

2. Colliders and Collision Detection
- **Definition**: Colliders define the physical boundaries of objects and enable collision detection, allowing objects to interact realistically.
- **Types of Colliders**:
- **Box, Sphere, and Capsule Colliders**: Simple colliders used for basic shapes.
- **Mesh Collider (Unity)** and **Complex Collision (Unreal)**: Used for complex, irregular shapes.
- **Implementing Collision Detection**:

- **Unity**:

```csharp
void OnCollisionEnter(Collision collision) {
Debug.Log("Collision detected with " + collision.gameObject.name);
}
```

- **Unreal**:

```cpp
void AMyActor::NotifyHit(UPrimitiveComponent* MyComp, AActor* Other, UPrimitiveComponent* OtherComp, bool bSelfMoved, FVector HitLocation, FVector HitNormal, FVector NormalImpulse, const FHitResult& Hit) {
UE_LOG(LogTemp, Warning, TEXT("Collision with %s"), *Other->GetName());
}
```

- **Explanation**: Both Unity and Unreal offer built-in methods for handling collision events, allowing developers to trigger specific responses based on interactions.

3. Triggers and Trigger Events
- **Definition**: Triggers are colliders that detect interactions without physically blocking objects. They're commonly used for area detection, events, and checkpoints.
- **Use Cases in Games**: Trigger zones are useful for activating events (e.g., pickups, damage zones) or initiating animations.
- **Example Implementation**:
- **Unity**:

```csharp
void OnTriggerEnter(Collider other) {
Debug.Log("Trigger entered by " + other.gameObject.name);
}
```

- **Unreal**:

```cpp
void AMyActor::NotifyActorBeginOverlap(AActor* OtherActor) {
UE_LOG(LogTemp, Warning, TEXT("Trigger activated by %s"),
*OtherActor->GetName());
}
```

- **Explanation**: These methods demonstrate how to detect trigger events in Unity and Unreal, making it possible to respond to character interactions.

—-

Encapsulating Physics Logic in OOP Design

1. Modularizing Physics with Object-Oriented Principles
- **Encapsulation**: Organize physics behaviors in self-contained classes to separate and manage game physics logic. For instance, separate classes could handle different object properties like movement, collision, and interaction logic.
- **Inheritance**: Use base classes to define common physics behaviors, and extend them for specific object types.
- **Example Structure**:
- **Base Physics Object**: Define common properties such as mass, friction, and collision response.
- **Specific Objects (e.g., Ball, Box)**: Inherit from the base object and override properties as needed.

2. Example of OOP-Driven Physics Class in Unity
- **Base Physics Object**:
```csharp
public class PhysicsObject : MonoBehaviour {
protected Rigidbody rb;
```

```csharp
protected virtual void Awake() {
    rb = gameObject.AddComponent();
}

public virtual void ApplyForce(Vector3 force) {
    rb.AddForce(force);
}
}
```
"

- **Derived Class for Specific Object**:
```csharp
public class Ball : PhysicsObject {
protected override void Awake() {
base.Awake();
rb.mass = 0.5f;
}

public override void ApplyForce(Vector3 force) {
    base.ApplyForce(force * 1.5f); // Custom behavior
}
}
```
"

- **Explanation**: This example demonstrates how to create a customizable base class for physics objects and extend it for specific types, promoting modular design.

—-

Project: Create Object Interactions for a Simple Physics-Based Game

Project Overview
- **Objective**: Develop a simple game where players interact with objects, triggering physics-based responses like collisions, rolling, or bouncing.

- **Core Features**:
- Implement rigidbodies, colliders, and triggers.
- Apply forces and simulate real-world interactions like gravity and friction.
- Use object-oriented programming to organize physics logic.

Step-by-Step Project Walkthrough

1. **Set Up a Basic Scene with Interactive Objects**
   - Create a basic scene with objects like a ball, box, and ramp.
   - Assign Rigidbody and Collider components to each object to enable physics responses.

2. **Implement Rigidbodies and Colliders**
   - Add Rigidbody components to each interactive object, adjusting mass and friction properties to control their behavior.
   - Code Example (Unity):
   ```csharp
   Rigidbody ballRb = ballObject.AddComponent();
   ballRb.mass = 1f;
   ballRb.drag = 0.5f; // Friction
   ```
   - Explanation: This setup allows objects to react naturally to physics forces and interact with the environment.

3. **Apply Forces and Add Interactivity**
   - **Player Interaction**: Implement methods to apply forces based on player input. For example, let the player push or kick objects.
   - Code Example (Apply Force to Ball):
   ```csharp
   if (Input.GetKeyDown(KeyCode.Space)) {
   ballRb.AddForce(Vector3.forward * 10f, ForceMode.Impulse);
   }
   ```

- **Explanation**: This lets players apply a directional force to an object, triggering movement and collision responses.

4. **Set Up Trigger Zones for Object Interactions**
   - **Objective**: Create trigger zones that activate effects like color changes or sounds upon contact.
   - **Implementation**: Add a collider and set it as a trigger, then write a script to detect when objects enter the trigger.
   - Code Example (Unity):

```csharp
void OnTriggerEnter(Collider other) {
if (other.CompareTag("Player")) {
gameObject.GetComponent().material.color = Color.red;
}
}
```

   - **Explanation**: This changes an object's color when the

player enters the trigger area, creating interactive feedback.

5. **Test Physics Interactions and Adjust Properties**
   - **Fine-Tune Object Properties**: Adjust Rigidbody settings, collider boundaries, and force values to ensure smooth, realistic interactions.
   - **Testing and Iteration**: Continuously test each component to achieve the desired effect. Balance forces and friction for a satisfying physics experience.

—-

Conclusion and Key Takeaways

- **Recap of Physics Fundamentals**: Summarize the role of Rigidbodies, Colliders, and Triggers in creating realistic interactions in game worlds.

Emphasize how object-oriented programming principles help organize and simplify complex physics behavior.

- **Highlight the Project**: The project reinforces core physics concepts, showing readers how to create interactive, physics-driven game elements. This provides a solid foundation for developing more advanced physics interactions in future games.

Chapter 11: Event-Driven Programming in Game Development

—-

Introduction to Event-Driven Programming in Games

- **Importance of Event-Driven Programming**: Events make game systems responsive and interactive by enabling communication between different game objects and components. This approach allows for flexible and modular gameplay mechanics, as objects can react to player actions, system changes, and environmental conditions.

 - **Objective of this Chapter**: Understand the fundamentals of events and delegates in C# (Unity) and event dispatchers in C++ (Unreal Engine), explore the use of event-driven design patterns in game systems, and apply these concepts through a hands-on project where a collectible system responds to player actions.

—-

Introduction to Events and Delegates (C#) / Event Dispatchers (C++)

1. Understanding Events and Delegates in C# (Unity)

- **What Are Events in C#?**: Events in C# are a way for one part of a program to communicate with another. They allow a class to publish an action, which other classes can subscribe to and respond to.
  - **Delegates and Their Role**: Delegates are type-safe references to methods. In event-driven programming, delegates act as pointers to event-handler methods, making it possible to call those methods when an event is triggered.
  - **Syntax and Structure**:
  - **Declaring a Delegate**:
```csharp
public delegate void ItemCollectedEventHandler();
```

  - **Declaring an Event**:
```csharp
public event ItemCollectedEventHandler OnItemCollected;
```

  - **Triggering an Event**:
```csharp
if (OnItemCollected != null) {
OnItemCollected();
}
```

  - **Explanation**: This setup shows how delegates work with events, enabling an object to notify other objects when an event occurs, like collecting an item.

2. Event Dispatchers in C++ (Unreal Engine)

- **Understanding Event Dispatchers**: Event dispatchers in Unreal Engine serve a similar purpose to events in Unity, enabling one class to broadcast an action and allowing other classes to respond to it.
  - **Creating an Event Dispatcher**:
  - **Declaration**:

```cpp
DECLARE_DYNAMIC_MULTICAST_DELEGATE(FOnItemCollected);
```

- **Defining an Event Dispatcher in a Class**:

```cpp
UPROPERTY(BlueprintAssignable)
FOnItemCollected OnItemCollected;
```

- **Broadcasting an Event**:

```cpp
OnItemCollected.Broadcast();
```

- **Explanation**: Unreal's event dispatchers are powerful tools for creating reactive systems, allowing developers to define custom events that other classes can handle.

3. Use Cases in Games
- **Triggering Reactions**: Events can trigger reactions across a variety of game scenarios, like scoring points, responding to player actions, and updating the UI.
- **Flexible Game Architecture**: Event-driven design leads to more modular and maintainable code, where changes to one system don't require changes to others.

—-

Creating Reactive and Interactive Game Environments

1. How Events Make Games Interactive

- **Dynamic World Reactions**: Events make it possible for the game world to react to player actions dynamically, such as enemies spawning after a certain item is collected or doors opening when all enemies are defeated.

- **Efficient Communication Between Objects**: Events minimize dependencies between objects, allowing them to interact without directly referencing each other. For example, an enemy can subscribe to a "PlayerDetected" event without knowing specifics about the player.
  - **Example Scenarios**:
  - **Player Health System**: When the player's health changes, an event can update the UI, trigger sounds, or even call an animation without altering each of these systems directly.
  - **Inventory System**: Collecting an item can trigger events that update the inventory, play sounds, and show animations simultaneously.

2. Setting Up Events for Real-Time Feedback

- **Using Delegates and Events for Immediate Feedback**: For actions like button presses, firing weapons, and item pickups, events provide real-time feedback without delay, improving gameplay responsiveness.
  - **Example in Unity**: Health System that triggers a UI update upon health reduction.
  ```csharp
  public delegate void HealthChanged(int currentHealth);
  public event HealthChanged OnHealthChanged;

  public void TakeDamage(int damage) {
    currentHealth -= damage;
    OnHealthChanged?.Invoke(currentHealth); // Trigger event
  }
  ```
  - **Explanation**: The event allows other components, like the UI, to react to changes in the player's health immediately.

—-

Event-Driven Design Patterns in Game Systems

1. Publisher-Subscriber Pattern

- **Overview**: The publisher-subscriber (pub-sub) pattern decouples objects from each other, allowing them to communicate through events. The publisher triggers an event, and any subscribers listen and react.
    - **Benefits**: Reduces coupling between classes, making systems modular and maintainable.
    - **Example**: A collectible system where an item triggers a "collected" event and various systems (score manager, inventory, UI) respond to it.
    - **Implementation**:
    - **Unity**:
    ```csharp
    public class ItemCollector : MonoBehaviour {
    public delegate void ItemCollected();
    public static event ItemCollected OnItemCollected;

    void Collect() {
      // Collect item logic
      OnItemCollected?.Invoke(); // Trigger event
      }
    }
    ```
    - **Subscriber**:
    ```csharp
    ItemCollector.OnItemCollected += UpdateScore; // Respond to event
    ```

2. Observer Pattern

- **Overview**: The observer pattern allows one object (the subject) to notify dependent objects (observers) of state changes without tightly coupling them.
    - **Use in Game Development**: Commonly used for notifying observers of events, like player position changes, inventory updates, or level transitions.

- **Example Use Case**: Observers like a health UI, sound manager, and achievement tracker all respond to changes in player health.

—-

Project: Building a Collectible System with Event Notifications

Project Overview

- **Objective**: Create a collectible system where objects like coins or power-ups trigger events upon collection. Subscribers, such as the score manager and UI, will respond to these events.
    - **Core Features**:
    - Implement an item class that triggers an "OnCollected" event.
    - Create listeners for the collectible event to update the player's score, display animations, and play sounds.
    - Use the publisher-subscriber pattern for managing multiple interactions in response to a single event.

Step-by-Step Project Walkthrough

1. **Define the Collectible Item Class**
    - **Unity Implementation**:
    - Declare a delegate and event for item collection:
```csharp
public class CollectibleItem : MonoBehaviour {
public delegate void ItemCollected();
public static event ItemCollected OnItemCollected;

void Collect() {
    // Collect item logic
    OnItemCollected?.Invoke(); // Trigger event
    Destroy(gameObject); // Remove item
```

```
}
}
"""
```

- **Explanation**: The event, 'OnItemCollected', is invoked when an item is collected, notifying any subscribers (e.g., score manager).

2. **Create Subscribers for the Collectible Event**

- **Subscriber: Score Manager**:

```csharp
public class ScoreManager : MonoBehaviour {
int score = 0;

void OnEnable() {
  CollectibleItem.OnItemCollected += IncreaseScore;
  }

void OnDisable() {
  CollectibleItem.OnItemCollected -= IncreaseScore;
  }

void IncreaseScore() {
  score += 10;
  Debug.Log("Score: " + score);
  }
  }
"""
```

- **Explanation**: The 'ScoreManager' listens to the 'OnItemCollected' event and increases the score whenever the event is triggered.

3. **Add Visual Feedback with UI Updates**

- **UI Update**: Add a UI component that responds to the collectible event to display a message or animate the score.

```csharp
public class UIManager : MonoBehaviour {
void OnEnable() {
CollectibleItem.OnItemCollected += DisplayMessage;
}

void OnDisable() {
CollectibleItem.OnItemCollected -= DisplayMessage;
}

void DisplayMessage() {
Debug.Log("Item Collected!");
// Code to update UI
}
}
```

- **Explanation**: The UI manager listens to the event and updates the UI, providing feedback to the player.

4. **Implement Sound Feedback**

- **Sound Manager**:
```csharp
public class SoundManager : MonoBehaviour {
public AudioClip collectSound;
public AudioSource audioSource;

void OnEnable() {
CollectibleItem.OnItemCollected += PlayCollectSound;
}

void OnDisable() {
```

```
CollectibleItem.OnItemCollected -= PlayCollectSound;
}

void PlayCollectSound() {
    audioSource.PlayOneShot(collectSound);
    }
}
```
"""

- **Explanation**: Sound manager subscribes to the collectible event, playing a sound when an item is collected, enhancing feedback.

5. **Testing the Event-Driven Collectible System**

- **Setup and Run**: Place collectible items in the scene, and ensure the score, UI, and sound managers respond correctly when items are collected.
    - **Debugging and Iteration**: Adjust collectible properties, add more subscribers if needed, and test for seamless interaction.

—-

Conclusion and Key Takeaways

- **Recap of Event-Driven Programming Benefits**: Event-driven programming allows for responsive, interactive, and modular game systems that are easy to maintain and scale.
    - **Project Reflection**: The collectible system illustrates how event-driven programming enables multiple game elements to react to player actions simultaneously, creating a dynamic and immersive game experience.

Chapter 12: Optimizing Performance in Object-Oriented Game Design

—-

Introduction to Performance Optimization in Games

- **Importance of Performance Optimization**: In modern game development, performance is crucial for player experience. Poor performance can lead to lag, frame rate drops, and overall frustration. Optimizing performance enhances gameplay and can broaden your game's accessibility on various platforms.
  - **Objective of this Chapter**: Identify common performance bottlenecks in game design, explore memory management techniques like object pooling and efficient code structuring, discuss resource management and scene transitions, and apply these concepts in a hands-on project focused on optimizing a simple shooter game.

—-

Identifying Common Performance Bottlenecks in Games

1. Understanding Performance Bottlenecks

- **Definition of Bottlenecks**: A performance bottleneck occurs when a particular component of a system limits the overall performance. Identifying and addressing these issues is vital for optimizing a game's performance.
  - **Common Types of Bottlenecks**:
  - **CPU Bottlenecks**: High CPU usage due to complex calculations, physics simulations, or excessive object updates can cause slowdowns.
  - **GPU Bottlenecks**: Rendering issues can arise from high polygon counts, complex shaders, or too many draw calls, leading to frame rate drops.
  - **Memory Bottlenecks**: Insufficient memory management can result in frequent garbage collection, causing stutters or crashes.

2. Analyzing Game Performance

- **Profiling Tools**: Utilize profiling tools like Unity Profiler, Unreal Insights, or other third-party solutions to analyze game performance.
  - **Key Metrics to Monitor**:
  - **Frame Rate (FPS)**: Measure the number of frames rendered per second.
  - **CPU and GPU Usage**: Track usage percentages to identify heavy loads.
  - **Memory Usage**: Monitor memory consumption and garbage collection events.

3. Common Issues Leading to Bottlenecks

- **High Object Count**: Having too many objects in a scene can overwhelm the system. Consider using fewer objects with instancing or LOD (Level of Detail) techniques.
  - **Complex AI Logic**: AI computations that run every frame can slow down the game. Consider simplifying algorithms or using state machines.
  - **Heavy Physics Calculations**: Too many physics objects or complex interactions can degrade performance. Use simplified colliders and reduce the number of physics updates.

- **Excessive Draw Calls**: Each object rendered increases draw calls, which can be costly. Batch static objects and use texture atlases to reduce draw calls.

—-

Memory Management, Object Pooling, and Efficient Code Structuring

1. Memory Management Techniques

- **Understanding Memory Allocation**: Dynamic memory allocation can lead to fragmentation and increased garbage collection. Pre-allocate memory where possible to minimize overhead.
  - **Garbage Collection**: Frequent garbage collection can cause frame rate drops. Reduce allocations in frequently called methods (e.g., Update() in Unity).
  - **Managing Game Assets**: Load and unload assets strategically. Use asynchronous loading techniques for large assets to prevent frame rate drops during gameplay.

2. Implementing Object Pooling

- **What is Object Pooling?**: Object pooling is a design pattern that reuses objects instead of instantiating and destroying them, minimizing memory allocations and garbage collection.
  - **Benefits of Object Pooling**:
  - **Performance Improvement**: Reduces the overhead of instantiation and destruction.
  - **Consistent Frame Rates**: Prevents stutters caused by garbage collection spikes.
  - **Implementing Object Pooling**:
  - **Creating an Object Pool**:

```csharp
public class ObjectPool where T : MonoBehaviour {
private Queue pool = new Queue();

public T Get() {
  if (pool.Count > 0) {
  return pool.Dequeue();
  } else {
  return InstantiateNewObject();
  }
  }

public void ReturnToPool(T obj) {
  pool.Enqueue(obj);
  }

private T InstantiateNewObject() {
  // Logic to instantiate a new object
  }
  }
```

- **Using the Pool**: Retrieve objects from the pool when needed and return them after use.

3. Efficient Code Structuring

- **Principles of Clean Code**: Follow SOLID principles (Single responsibility, Open/closed, Liskov substitution, Interface segregation, Dependency inversion) to write maintainable and efficient code.
  - **Reducing Complexity**: Keep methods short and focused, minimize dependencies between classes, and use clear naming conventions for readability.
  - **Using Design Patterns**: Implement appropriate design patterns (e.g.,

Singleton, Factory, State) to manage complexity and improve performance.

—-

Managing Resources and Scene Transitions

1. Resource Management Strategies

- **Loading Assets Efficiently**: Use asynchronous loading to manage assets without interrupting gameplay. Implement loading screens for larger scenes to hide loading times.
  - **Memory Profiling**: Continuously monitor memory usage during development to identify memory leaks or excessive usage.

2. Scene Management Techniques

- **Loading and Unloading Scenes**: Use additive scene loading in Unity to manage large game worlds. This allows for smoother transitions between areas without heavy loading times.
  - **Scene Transition Optimization**: Implement smooth transitions using fade effects or loading animations to enhance player experience.
  - **Example Code for Scene Management**:

```csharp
public class SceneLoader : MonoBehaviour {
public void LoadScene(string sceneName) {
StartCoroutine(LoadAsync(sceneName));
}

private IEnumerator LoadAsync(string sceneName) {
AsyncOperation operation = SceneManager.LoadSceneAsync(sceneName);
    while (!operation.isDone) {
    // Show loading progress
```

```
yield return null;
}
}
}
```
"""

- **Explanation**: The above code demonstrates a coroutine to load scenes asynchronously, enhancing performance during transitions.

—-

Project: Optimizing a Simple Shooter Game Using Object Pooling

Project Overview

- **Objective**: Optimize a simple shooter game by implementing object pooling for projectiles and enemies, improving performance, and maintaining a smooth frame rate during gameplay.
    - **Core Features**:
    - Create a pool for projectiles.
    - Implement pooling for enemy characters.
    - Ensure efficient memory usage and frame rate stability.

Step-by-Step Project Walkthrough

1. **Define the Projectile Class**

- **Projectile Script**:
    ```csharp
    public class Projectile : MonoBehaviour {
    public float speed;
    public float lifetime;

    void Update() {
    ```

```csharp
transform.Translate(Vector3.forward * speed * Time.deltaTime);
lifetime -= Time.deltaTime;
if (lifetime <= 0) {
ReturnToPool();
}
}

void ReturnToPool() {
ObjectPool.Instance.ReturnToPool(this);
}
}
"""
```

- **Explanation**: The projectile moves forward and returns to the pool when its lifetime expires, preventing excess object instantiation.

2. **Implement the Object Pool for Projectiles**

- **Projectile Pool**:
```csharp
public class ProjectilePool : MonoBehaviour {
public Projectile projectilePrefab;
private Queue pool = new Queue();

public Projectile Get() {
if (pool.Count > 0) {
return pool.Dequeue();
}
return Instantiate(projectilePrefab);
}

public void ReturnToPool(Projectile projectile) {
pool.Enqueue(projectile);
projectile.gameObject.SetActive(false);
```

```
}
}
"""
```

- **Explanation**: This pool manages projectile instances, reusing them instead of instantiating new ones.

3. **Implement Shooting Logic Using the Pool**

- **Player Shooting Script**:
```csharp
public class PlayerShooter : MonoBehaviour {
public ProjectilePool projectilePool;

void Update() {
if (Input.GetButtonDown("Fire1")) {
Shoot();
}
}

void Shoot() {
    Projectile projectile = projectilePool.Get();
    projectile.transform.position = transform.position; // Set position
    projectile.gameObject.SetActive(true); // Activate projectile
    }
}
"""
```

- **Explanation**: The player script retrieves a projectile from the pool when firing, enhancing performance by avoiding instantiation.

4. **Optimize Enemy Management with Object Pooling**

- **Enemy Pooling**:
```csharp
"""csharp
```

```csharp
public class Enemy : MonoBehaviour {
public float health;

public void TakeDamage(float damage) {
  health -= damage;
  if (health <= 0) {
  ReturnToPool();
  }
  }

void ReturnToPool() {
  EnemyPool.Instance.ReturnToPool(this);
  }
  }
  "'
```

5. **Create the Enemy Pool Class**

- **Enemy Pool**:

```csharp
public class EnemyPool : MonoBehaviour {
public Enemy enemyPrefab;
private Queue pool = new Queue();

public Enemy Get() {
  if (pool.Count > 0) {
  return pool.Dequeue();
  }
  return Instantiate(enemyPrefab);
  }

public void ReturnToPool(Enemy enemy) {
  pool.Enqueue(enemy);
```

```
enemy.gameObject.SetActive(false);
}
}
```
```

- **Explanation**: This enemy pool reuses enemy instances, minimizing overhead from frequent inst

antiation.

6. **Testing and Debugging**

- **Setup Testing Environment**: Create a simple level with spawning enemies and a player shooter.
  - **Monitor Performance**: Use profiling tools to monitor frame rates and memory usage.
  \- **Iterate Based on Feedback**: Adjust pooling sizes, enemy spawn rates, and projectile speeds based on performance metrics.

—-

### **Conclusion: Key Takeaways and Future Considerations**

- **Summary of Optimization Techniques**: Understanding performance bottlenecks and implementing object pooling are essential for creating smooth and responsive games.
  - **Reflection on Project**: The hands-on project illustrates the practical benefits of object pooling, demonstrating significant improvements in performance and memory management in the shooter game.
  - **Looking Ahead**: As game development continues to evolve, staying updated with the latest optimization techniques and tools is crucial. Consider exploring multithreading, asynchronous programming, and other advanced optimization strategies to further enhance game performance.
```

—-

Final Thoughts

- **Encouragement to Experiment**: Encourage readers to apply these optimization techniques to their projects and continue learning about performance management in game design.
  - **Resources for Further Learning**: Provide links to books, articles, and video tutorials focused on performance optimization and object-oriented programming in game development.

—-

This outline provides a comprehensive structure for Chapter 12, focusing on optimizing performance through object-oriented design in game development. Each section can be expanded upon with specific examples, illustrations, and in-depth explanations to achieve the target word count of 7000 words.

Chapter 13: Debugging and Testing OOP-Based Game Code

—-

Introduction to Debugging and Testing in Game Development

- **Importance of Debugging and Testing**: Debugging and testing are critical phases in game development. They ensure that the game functions correctly and provides a smooth experience for players. A game with bugs can lead to negative reviews and loss of player engagement.
  - **Objective of this Chapter**: This chapter will cover essential debugging techniques, tools for debugging in Unity and Unreal Engine, writing unit tests for gameplay elements, and a hands-on project to set up and test a basic game loop using debugging tools.

—-

Essential Debugging Techniques for Game Development

1. Understanding Debugging in Game Development

- **Definition of Debugging**: Debugging is the process of identifying,

isolating, and fixing problems or bugs within code. It is crucial to ensure that the game runs as intended.
  - **Common Types of Bugs**:
  - **Logic Errors**: Issues where the code runs but does not produce the expected outcome.
  - **Runtime Errors**: Errors that occur while the game is running, often leading to crashes.
  - **Performance Issues**: Problems that result in low frame rates or lag.

2. Basic Debugging Techniques

- **Code Review**: Regularly review your code with peers or through self-analysis to catch potential bugs early.
  - **Print Statements**: Use 'Debug.Log()' in Unity or 'UE_LOG' in Unreal to output variable states and flow of execution to the console.
  - **Assertions**: Implement assertions in your code to validate assumptions. Use 'Debug.Assert()' in Unity to catch unexpected states.

—-

Using Breakpoints, Profilers, and Logging in Unity and Unreal

1. Utilizing Breakpoints

- **What are Breakpoints?**: Breakpoints are markers set in the code that pause execution, allowing you to inspect variables and the call stack.
  - **Setting Breakpoints in Unity**:
  - Use Visual Studio or Rider to set breakpoints.
  - Explanation of how to inspect variables and step through code.
  - **Setting Breakpoints in Unreal**:
  - Use the built-in debugger in the Unreal Editor.
  - Explanation of inspecting object properties and stepping through Blueprints.

2. Profiling Game Performance

- **Importance of Profiling**: Profiling helps identify performance bottlenecks and optimize game performance.
    - **Unity Profiler**:
    - Overview of the Unity Profiler window.
    - Tracking CPU, GPU usage, memory allocations, and more.
    - **Unreal Insights**:
    - Introduction to Unreal Insights for profiling performance.
    - Understanding frame timings, memory usage, and identifying slow frames.

3. Logging for Debugging

- **Importance of Logging**: Logging provides a historical record of events and errors, which is invaluable for debugging.
    - **Implementing Logging in Unity**:
    - How to use 'Debug.Log()', 'Debug.LogWarning()', and 'Debug.LogError()'.
    - Best practices for logging (e.g., avoiding excessive logging).
    - **Implementing Logging in Unreal**:
    - Overview of 'UE_LOG' macros.
    - Best practices for logging in Unreal Engine, including categories and verbosity levels.

Writing Unit Tests for Key Components and Gameplay Elements

1. Understanding Unit Testing

- **Definition of Unit Testing**: Unit testing involves testing individual components or classes of the codebase to ensure they work as expected in isolation.

142

- **Benefits of Unit Testing**:
- Identifies issues early in development.
- Facilitates code refactoring.
- Improves overall code quality.

2. Writing Unit Tests in Unity

- **Setting Up Unity Test Framework**: Overview of the Unity Test Framework and how to integrate it into a project.
  - **Example Unit Test**:
  - Creating a simple unit test for a player health component:
```csharp
using NUnit.Framework;
using UnityEngine;

public class PlayerHealthTests {
    private PlayerHealth playerHealth;

[SetUp]
    public void SetUp() {
    playerHealth = new PlayerHealth(100);
    }

[Test]
    public void TakeDamage_ShouldReduceHealth() {
    playerHealth.TakeDamage(20);
    Assert.AreEqual(80, playerHealth.CurrentHealth);
    }
}
```

3. Writing Unit Tests in Unreal

- **Setting Up Unit Tests in Unreal**: Overview of how to set up unit tests using the Automation Framework in Unreal Engine.
  - **Example Unit Test**:
  - Creating a simple unit test for a character's health component:

```cpp
#include "Misc/AutomationTest.h"
#include "MyCharacter.h"

IMPLEMENT_SIMPLE_AUTOMATION_TEST(FMyCharacterTest, "GameTests.MyCharacterTest", EAutomationTestFlags::EditorContext | EAutomationTestFlags::SmokeTest)

bool FMyCharacterTest::RunTest(const FString& Parameters) {
    AMyCharacter* Character = NewObject();
    Character->SetHealth(100);
    Character->TakeDamage(20);
    TestEqual("Health should reduce correctly", Character->GetCurrentHealth(), 80);
    return true;
}
```

—-

Project: Setting Up and Testing a Basic Game Loop with Debugging Tools

Project Overview

- **Objective**: Create a simple game loop and implement debugging tools to test key components.
  - **Core Features**:
  - A player character that can move and take damage.

- Debugging through breakpoints, logging, and unit tests.

Step-by-Step Project Walkthrough

1. **Setting Up the Basic Game Loop**

- **Creating the Player Class**:
    - Outline a simple player class with health and movement functionality.
    - Sample code snippet:

```csharp
public class Player : MonoBehaviour {
public float speed = 5f;
public float health = 100f;

void Update() {
  Move();
  CheckHealth();
  }

void Move() {
  float horizontal = Input.GetAxis("Horizontal");
  float vertical = Input.GetAxis("Vertical");
  Vector3 direction = new Vector3(horizontal, 0, vertical).normalized;
  transform.Translate(direction * speed * Time.deltaTime);
  }

void CheckHealth() {
  if (health <= 0) {
  Debug.Log("Player is dead!");
  }
  }

public void TakeDamage(float amount) {
```

```
health -= amount;
Debug.Log($"Player took {amount} damage. Current health: {health}");
    }
}
"""
```

2. **Implementing Debugging Tools**

- **Using Breakpoints**:
    - Set breakpoints in the 'TakeDamage' method and the 'CheckHealth' method to inspect player health changes.
    - **Logging Player Actions**:
    - Use 'Debug.Log' to output player movement and health changes in the console.

3. **Writing Unit Tests for Player Functionality**

- **Testing Player Movement**:
    - Write a unit test to ensure that movement inputs correctly adjust the player's position.
    - **Testing Health Mechanics**:
    - Write unit tests for the 'TakeDamage' method to verify that health is reduced appropriately.

4. **Testing and Debugging the Game Loop**

- **Running Tests**:
    - Execute unit tests in Unity and verify outcomes.
    - **Debugging Live Gameplay**:
    - Play the game in the editor, using breakpoints and logs to check for any unexpected behavior or bugs.
    - **Profiling Performance**:
    - Use the Unity Profiler to monitor the game's performance during

gameplay, ensuring there are no significant frame drops or memory issues.

—-

Conclusion: Key Takeaways and Future Considerations

- **Summary of Debugging and Testing Techniques**: This chapter covered essential debugging techniques and tools, as well as unit testing to ensure robust game development.
    - **Reflection on Project**: The hands-on project illustrates how to integrate debugging tools into a simple game loop, enabling developers to identify and fix issues early in development.
    - **Looking Ahead**: As game complexity increases, continuous integration and automated testing should be explored. Familiarize yourself with advanced debugging techniques and tools to further enhance game quality.

—-

Final Thoughts

- **Encouragement to Experiment**: Encourage readers to apply these debugging techniques in their own projects and explore unit testing as a method to maintain high code quality.
    - **Resources for Further Learning**: Provide links to additional resources on debugging and testing in game development, such as books, articles, and online courses.

—-

This outline provides a comprehensive structure for Chapter 13, focusing on debugging and testing OOP-based game code. Each section can be expanded upon with specific examples, illustrations, and in-depth explanations to achieve the target word count of 7000 words.

Chapter 14: Final Project – Creating a Cohesive Game from Start to Finish

—-

Introduction to the Final Project

- **Purpose of the Final Project**: This chapter will guide you through the process of creating a cohesive game, applying all the knowledge gained in previous chapters on object-oriented programming (OOP), design patterns, debugging, and testing.
    - **Project Options**: You will choose between building a 2D platformer or an RPG, allowing for flexibility based on your interests and skill level.

—-

Project Overview and Scope: Building a 2D Platformer or RPG Game

1. Choosing Your Game Genre

- **2D Platformer Overview**: Discuss the characteristics of a 2D platformer, including level design, player mechanics (jumping, running), and enemies.

- **RPG Overview**: Discuss the key elements of RPGs, such as character progression, quests, inventory systems, and story development.

2. Defining the Game Concept

- **Game Title and Theme**: Brainstorm potential titles and themes for your game.
  - **Target Audience**: Identify the target audience for your game, considering age group, interests, and gaming habits.
  - **Game Features**: Outline the core features of your game, such as:
  - **For 2D Platformer**:
  - Level progression
  - Power-ups
  - Enemy types
  - **For RPG**:
  - Character customization
  - Quest system
  - Dialogue trees

3. Creating a Game Design Document (GDD)

- **Purpose of a GDD**: Explain the importance of a GDD in guiding the development process and keeping the project organized.
  - **Key Sections of the GDD**:
  - Game overview
  - Gameplay mechanics
  - Art style and sound design
  - Technical requirements
  - Project timeline and milestones

—-

Applying All Core OOP Principles and Design Patterns

1. Core OOP Principles

- **Encapsulation**: Discuss how encapsulation is used in your game to manage complexity. Provide examples of classes, such as 'Player', 'Enemy', and 'Item', that encapsulate data and behavior.
    - **Inheritance**: Explain how inheritance can simplify code reuse. Create base classes, like 'Character', and derive 'Player' and 'Enemy' from it.
    - **Polymorphism**: Demonstrate how polymorphism allows for flexible code, using interfaces or abstract classes. For example, implement an 'IAttackable' interface for characters that can be attacked.

2. Design Patterns in Game Development

- **Singleton Pattern**: Use a singleton for managing game states (e.g., 'GameManager').
    - **Observer Pattern**: Implement the observer pattern for event handling, such as player health changes notifying the UI to update.
    - **Factory Pattern**: Utilize the factory pattern to create game objects, like enemies or power-ups, based on certain criteria.
    - **State Machine Pattern**: Apply the state machine pattern for character behaviors (e.g., idle, walking, jumping for the player or patrolling, chasing, attacking for enemies).

3. Structuring Your Code

- **Organizing Your Project**: Discuss folder structures and organization for assets, scripts, and scenes. Consider using namespaces for better code management.
    - **Documenting Code**: Highlight the importance of code comments and documentation for maintaining clarity and facilitating teamwork.

—-

Finalizing Art, Sound, and User Experience

1. Art Design

- **Art Style Consistency**: Choose an art style (pixel art, cartoonish, realistic) that matches your game's theme and audience.
  - **Creating or Sourcing Assets**:
  - Use tools like Aseprite or Photoshop for custom sprite creation.
  - Consider using asset stores or open-source resources for sprites, backgrounds, and UI elements.

2. Sound Design

- **Sound Effects and Music**: Discuss the importance of sound in enhancing gameplay experience. Source or create sound effects for actions (jumping, collecting items) and background music.
  - **Implementing Audio in Unity/Unreal**:
  - **Unity**: Use the AudioSource component and AudioMixer to manage sound.
  - **Unreal**: Utilize the Sound Cue system to create dynamic audio experiences.

3. User Experience (UX) Design

- **User Interface Design**: Discuss principles of effective UI design, focusing on clarity and usability.
  - **Creating Menus and HUD**: Implement main menus, pause menus, and in-game HUD elements displaying health, score, and inventory.
  - **User Feedback**: Incorporate visual and auditory feedback for player actions (e.g., button presses, item pickups).

—-

Polishing, Debugging, and Preparing for Launch

1. Polishing the Game

- **Fine-Tuning Gameplay**: Iterate on gameplay based on testing feedback. Adjust difficulty, pacing, and player progression.
  - **Visual Polish**: Add particle effects, animations, and other visual enhancements to improve aesthetics.
  - **Sound Refinement**: Balance sound levels and ensure smooth transitions between different audio states.

2. Debugging the Game

- **Debugging Techniques Recap**: Revisit techniques learned in previous chapters, focusing on:
  - Using breakpoints to inspect game state.
  - Employing logging to track events and errors.
  - Utilizing profilers to ensure smooth performance.
  - **Testing Gameplay**: Conduct thorough playtesting sessions to identify bugs and gameplay issues. Gather feedback from a focus group or beta testers.

3. Preparing for Launch

- **Final Testing and QA**: Perform quality assurance testing to catch remaining bugs. Ensure compatibility across target platforms.
  - **Building the Game**: Create builds for different platforms (PC, console, mobile) and prepare the necessary files for distribution.
  - **Marketing and Distribution**:
  - Develop a marketing strategy to promote your game.
  - Choose distribution platforms (Steam, itch.io, App Store) and prepare necessary promotional materials (trailers, screenshots).

—-

Conclusion: Reflecting on the Game Development Journey

- **Summarizing Key Learning Points**: Reflect on the knowledge and skills acquired throughout the project, emphasizing the importance of OOP principles and design patterns.
    - **Celebrating Achievements**: Encourage readers to celebrate their accomplishments upon completing the project and to take pride in their work.
    - **Future Development Path**: Suggest exploring advanced topics in game development, such as networked multiplayer, VR/AR, or game monetization strategies.

—-

Final Thoughts

- **Encouragement to Share**: Motivate readers to share their completed games with the community and gather feedback for future improvements.
    - **Resources for Continued Learning**: Provide links to further resources, online courses, forums, and communities where readers can continue learning and growing as game developers.

—-

This outline provides a comprehensive structure for Chapter 14, focusing on creating a cohesive game from start to finish. Each section can be expanded upon with specific examples, illustrations, and in-depth explanations to achieve the target word count of 7000 words.

Conclusion: Advancing Your Skills Beyond This Book

As you reach the end of this book, it's essential to reflect on your journey through the intricacies of object-oriented programming (OOP) in game development. The knowledge and skills you've acquired provide a solid foundation for creating engaging, robust games. However, game development is a dynamic field, continually evolving with new technologies and methodologies. This conclusion aims to guide you in advancing your skills, exploring additional resources, and networking effectively within the gaming community.

Summary of Key Concepts and Tools Learned

Throughout this book, you have learned several critical concepts and tools that form the backbone of successful game development:

1. **Object-Oriented Programming Principles**: You've gained an understanding of core OOP principles—encapsulation, inheritance, and polymorphism. These principles enable you to write modular, reusable, and maintainable code, making your game easier to manage and expand.

2. **Design Patterns**: You explored various design patterns commonly used in game development, such as the Singleton, Observer, Factory, and

State Machine patterns. Understanding these patterns will help you structure your code more effectively and address common programming challenges.

3. **Game Design and Development Processes**: From initial concept through to final polishing, you've navigated the game development life cycle, including creating a game design document (GDD), building and refining gameplay mechanics, and preparing your game for launch.

4. **Debugging and Testing**: You learned essential debugging techniques, including the use of breakpoints, logging, and profiling. Moreover, you explored writing unit tests to ensure your code functions correctly, which is crucial for maintaining code quality.

5. **Art and Sound Integration**: You understood the importance of cohesive art and sound design in enhancing the player experience. You've seen how these elements can be effectively integrated into your game.

6. **Performance Optimization**: Techniques for identifying and resolving performance bottlenecks were discussed, ensuring your game runs smoothly on various platforms.

These foundational elements will not only assist you in your current projects but will also serve as a launchpad for more advanced exploration in game development.

—-

Exploring Further Resources and Advanced Topics

While this book provides a comprehensive introduction to OOP-based game development, many resources are available for further learning:

1. **Online Courses and Tutorials**:

- Platforms like **Udemy**, **Coursera**, and **Pluralsight** offer specialized courses on advanced game development topics, covering everything from AI programming to advanced graphics techniques.
- **YouTube** has countless channels dedicated to game development, featuring tutorials, live coding sessions, and developer talks.

2. **Books**:
- "Game Programming Patterns" by Robert Nystrom provides a deep dive into design patterns specifically tailored for game development.
- "The Art of Game Design: A Book of Lenses" by Jesse Schell explores the creative aspects of game design.

3. **Forums and Communities**:
- Join online communities such as **GameDev.net**, **Unity Forums**, or **Unreal Engine Forums** to connect with other developers, share your projects, and seek advice.
- **Reddit** has numerous subreddits like r/gamedev and r/indiegames, where you can find resources, discussions, and support from fellow game developers.

4. **Advanced Topics**: Consider delving into:
- **Networking and Multiplayer**: Explore how to implement networked gameplay, a key feature in many modern games.
- **Virtual Reality (VR) and Augmented Reality (AR)**: Learn how to develop for these immersive platforms, which are rapidly growing in popularity.
- **Artificial Intelligence (AI)**: Investigate AI techniques to create more engaging and challenging opponents and NPCs.
- **Game Monetization Strategies**: Understand various monetization models, including in-app purchases, subscriptions, and ads.

By continuously expanding your knowledge and skills, you'll remain competitive and innovative in the ever-changing landscape of game development.

—-

Tips for Networking and Growing as a Game Developer

Networking is an invaluable aspect of growing as a game developer. Building connections can lead to collaboration opportunities, mentorship, and even job offers. Here are some effective strategies for networking:

1. **Attend Game Development Conferences**: Participate in industry events such as the Game Developers Conference (GDC), PAX, or local game jams. These events provide opportunities to meet industry professionals, attend workshops, and showcase your work.

2. **Engage in Online Communities**: Actively participate in forums and social media groups dedicated to game development. Share your projects, seek feedback, and offer help to others. Being a part of the community can open doors to collaboration and support.

3. **Create a Portfolio**: Build a strong portfolio showcasing your best projects, including your final game from this book. A well-documented portfolio highlights your skills and creativity, making it easier for potential employers or collaborators to see your capabilities.

4. **Utilize Social Media**: Share your development journey on platforms like Twitter, Instagram, or LinkedIn. Use relevant hashtags (#gamedev, #indiedev) to increase visibility. Engaging with other developers and industry professionals can help expand your network.

5. **Join Local Game Development Groups**: Look for local meetups or clubs focused on game development. These groups can provide valuable networking opportunities and a chance to learn from peers in your area.

6. **Seek Mentorship**: Find experienced developers willing to mentor you.

A mentor can provide guidance, industry insights, and valuable feedback on your work, helping you navigate your career path more effectively.

Networking is about building genuine relationships. Be open to sharing your knowledge and helping others, as this can lead to meaningful connections in the long run.

—-

Acknowledgments and Next Steps

As you conclude your journey through this book, it's important to acknowledge the resources and communities that have contributed to your growth:

- **Authors and Developers**: Thank those whose works inspired and educated you throughout this process, from books and tutorials to influential game developers.
    - **Game Development Communities**: Appreciate the online forums and local groups that foster collaboration, support, and encouragement among developers.

Next Steps:
    - **Implement Your Learning**: Start working on your own game projects, applying the skills and concepts you've learned. Don't be afraid to experiment and innovate.
    - **Seek Feedback**: Share your projects with others, seek constructive criticism, and learn from feedback. Engaging with your audience can provide new perspectives and ideas for improvement.
    - **Keep Learning**: Continue exploring new technologies, trends, and best practices in game development. Lifelong learning is key to remaining relevant and successful in this field.

In conclusion, you have embarked on a rewarding journey into game development. As you advance your skills beyond this book, remember that the gaming industry thrives on creativity, collaboration, and passion. Embrace the challenges and joys of game development, and most importantly, have fun creating immersive experiences that entertain and inspire players around the world.

www.ingramcontent.com/pod-product-compliance
Lightning Source LLC
LaVergne TN
LVHW051340050326
832903LV00031B/3657